"That love is inexhaustible, you will be there" forever

THIS BOOK Belongs to

Visit Our Author Page At

amazon.com

Scan me

Black Rose PRESS HOUSE

THANKSGIVING COLORING BOOK

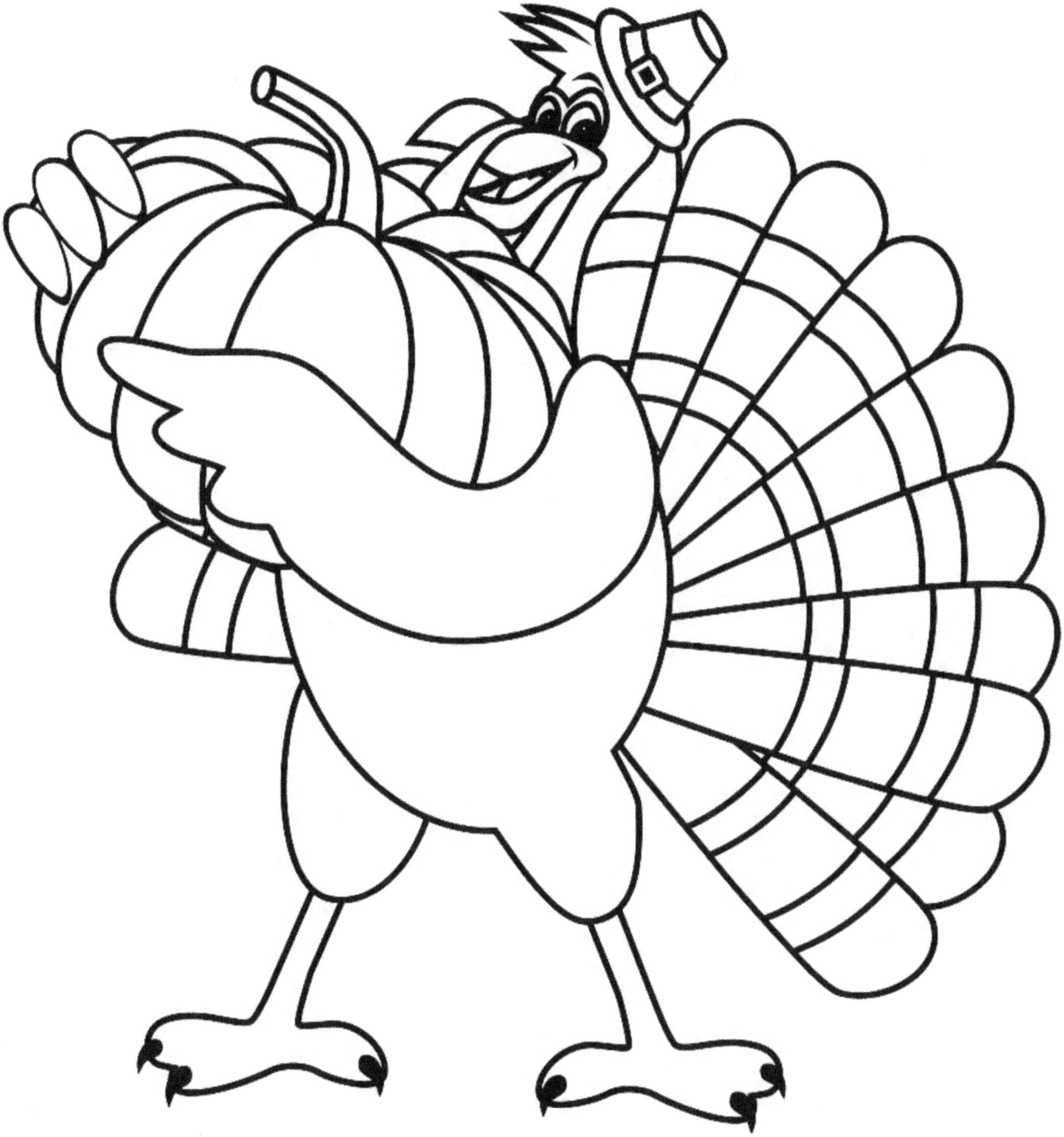

THANKSGIVING COLORING BOOK

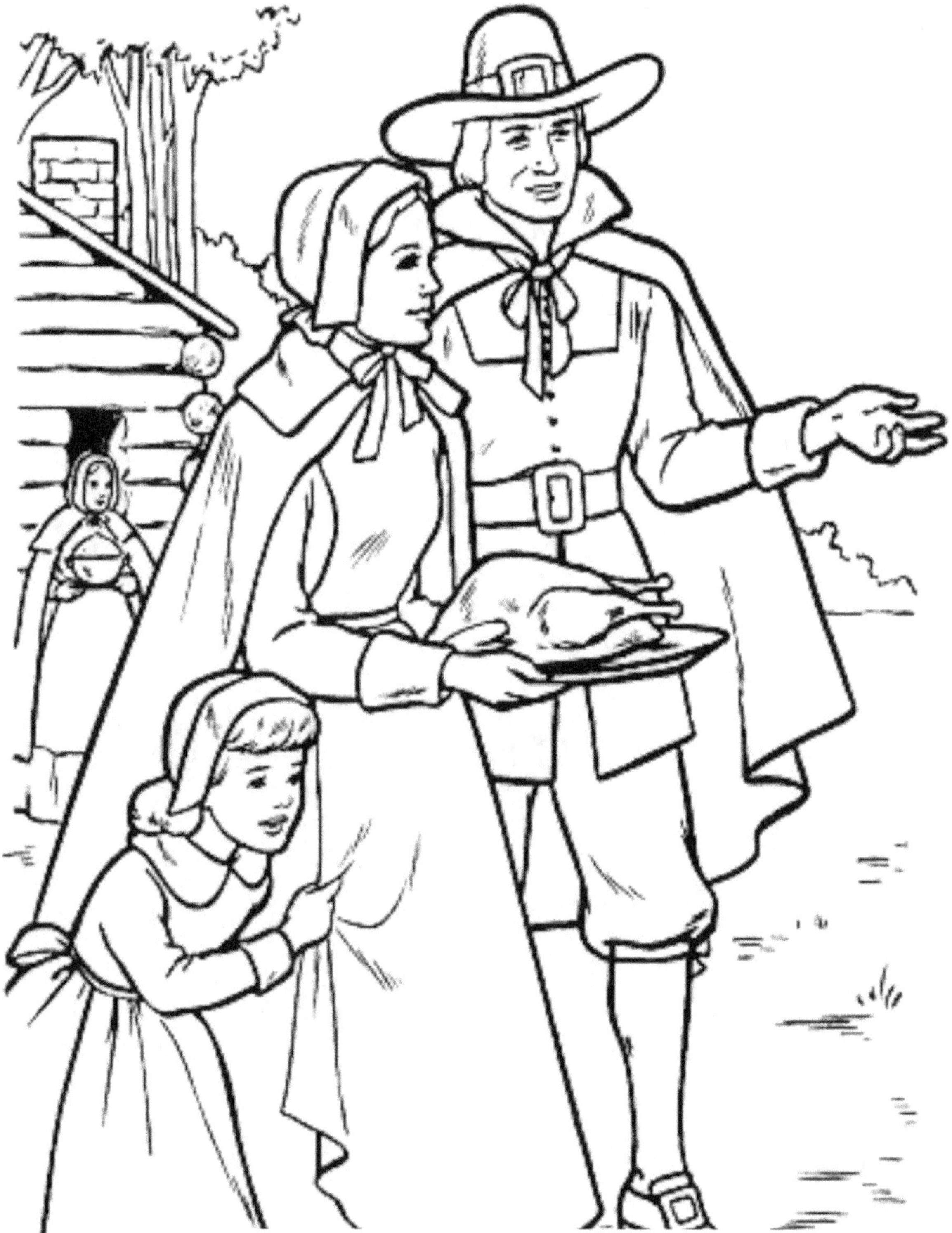

THANKSGIVING COLORING BOOK

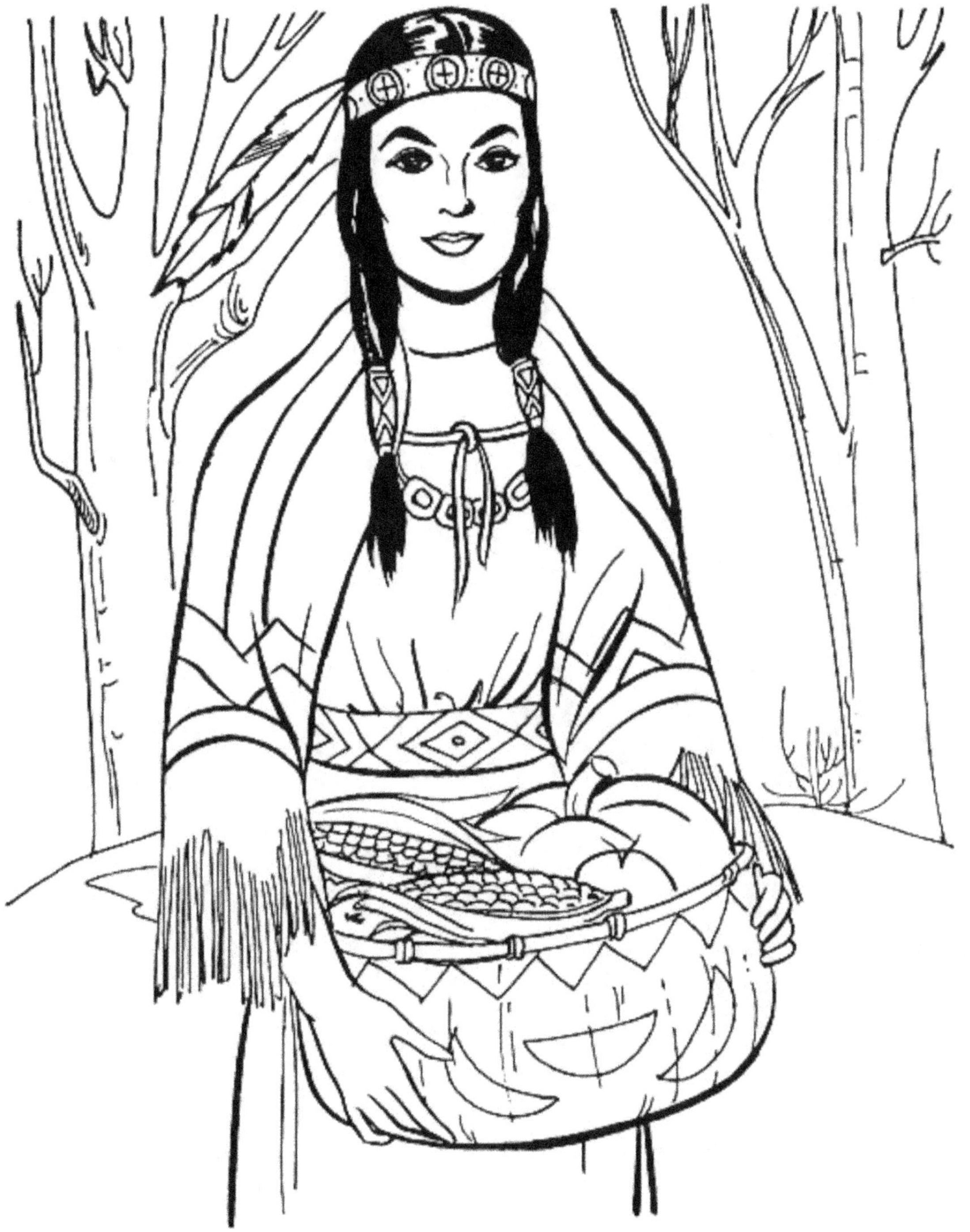

THANKSGIVING COLORING BOOK

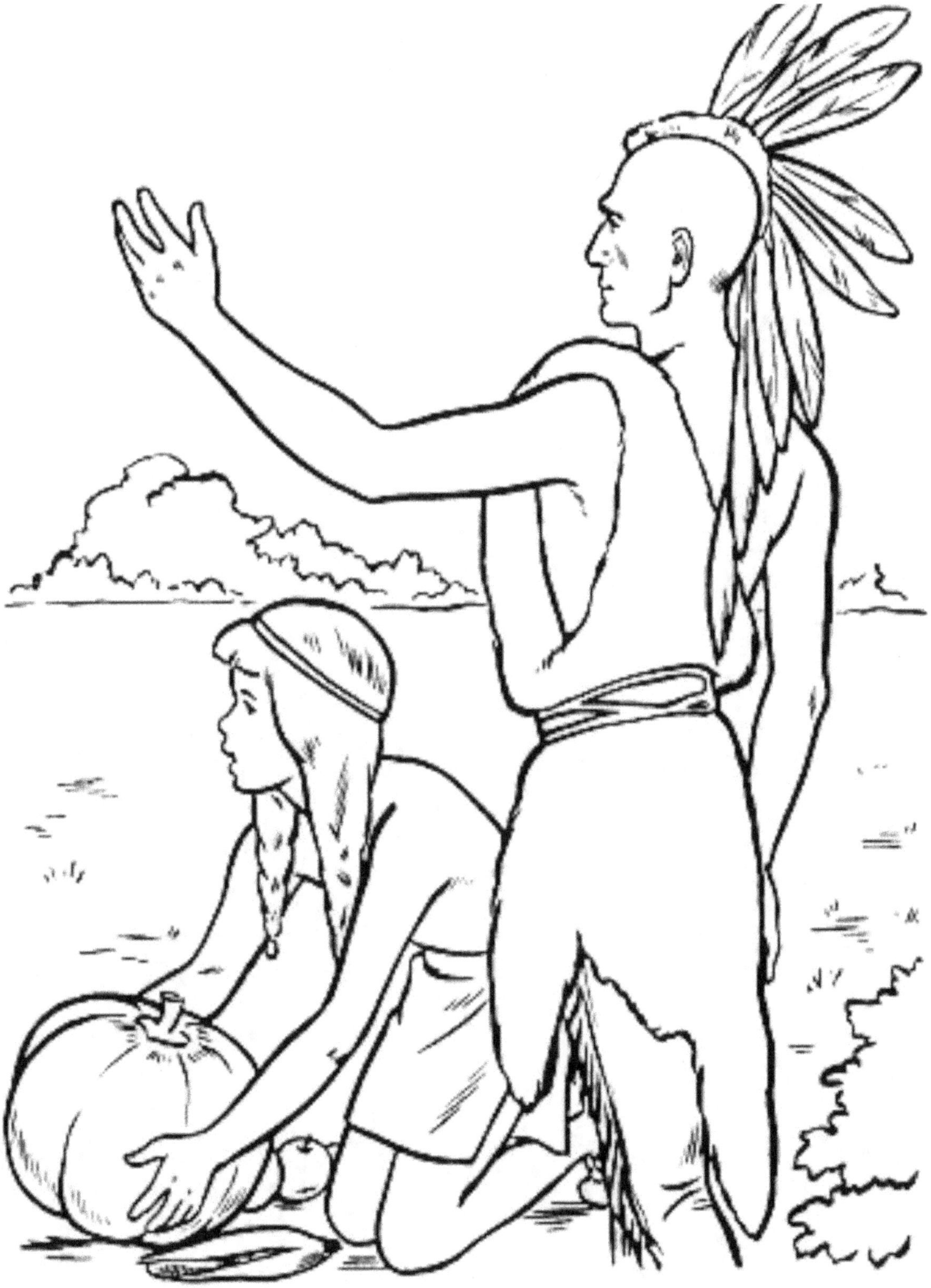

THANKSGIVING COLORING BOOK

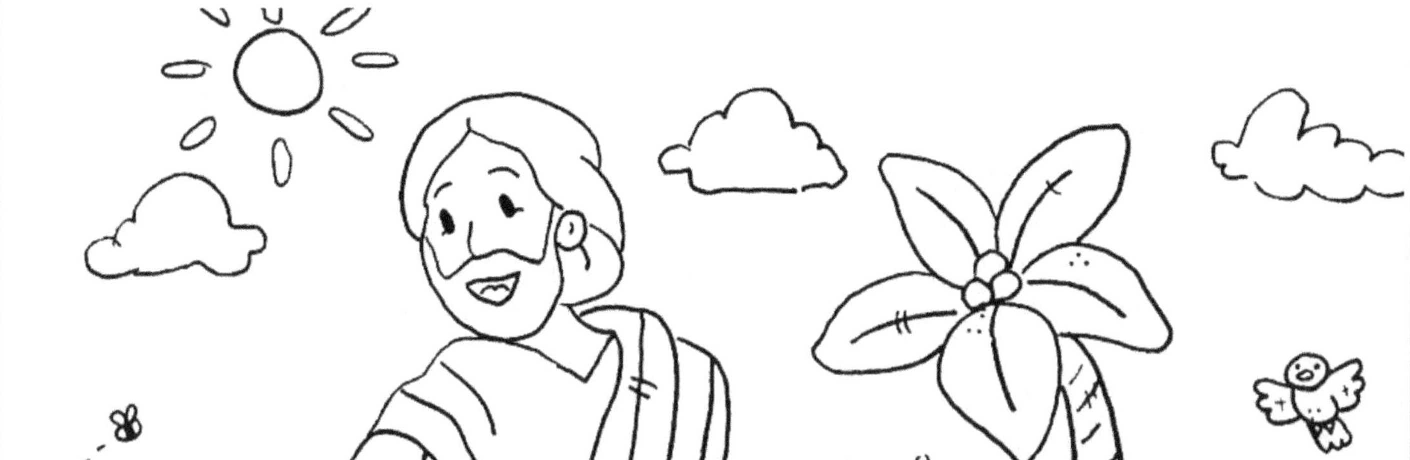

THANKSGIVING COLORING BOOK

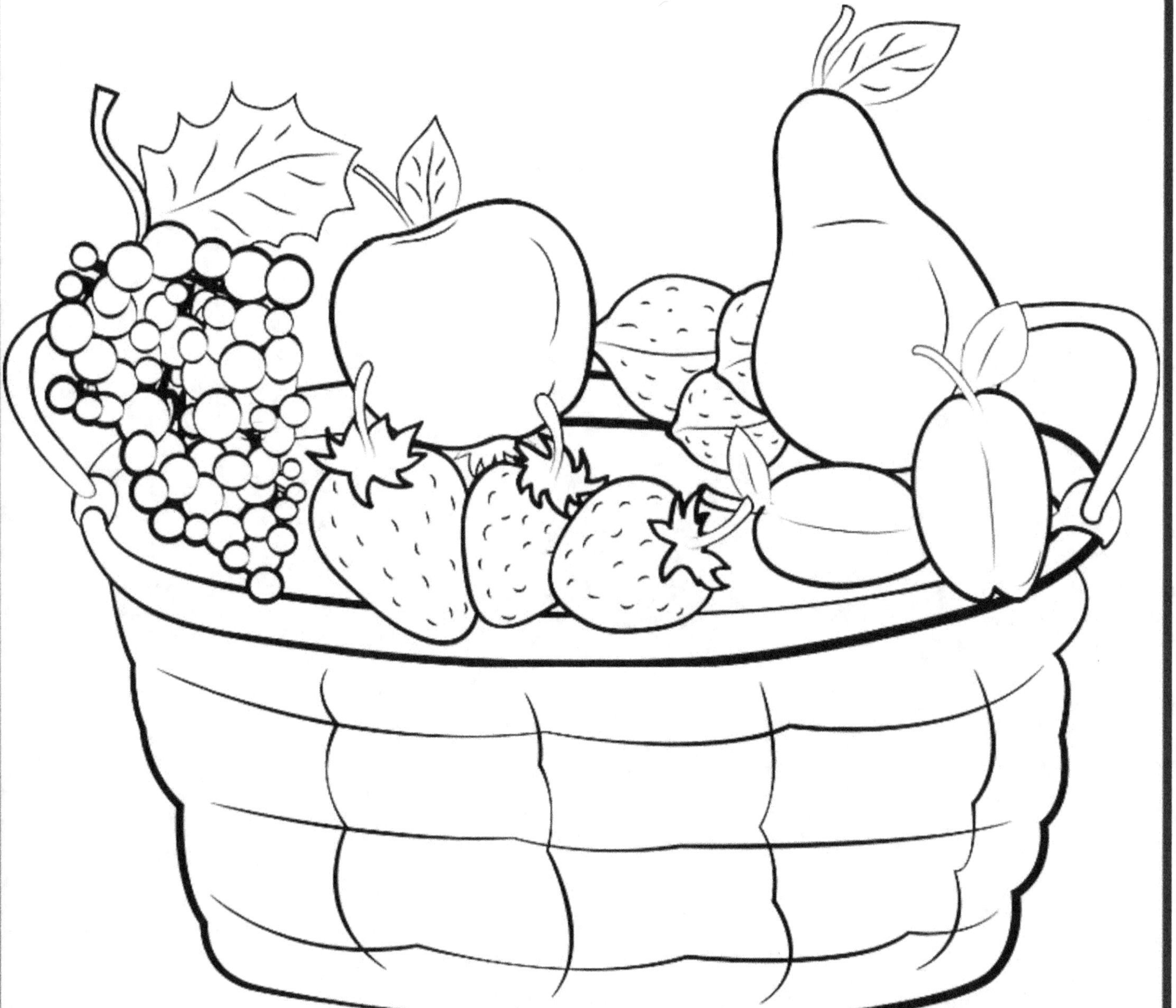

THANKSGIVING COLORING BOOK

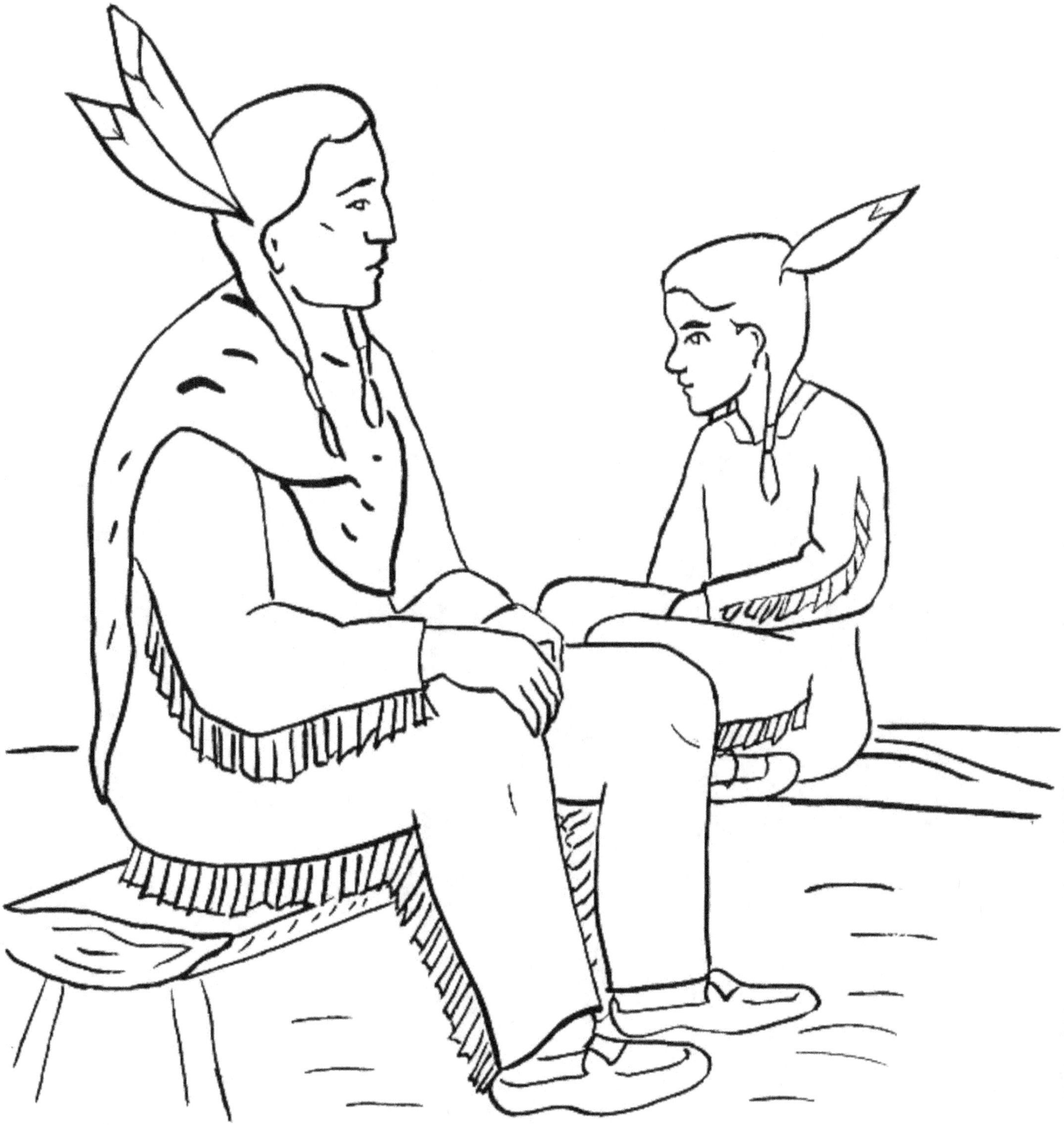

THANKSGIVING COLORING BOOK

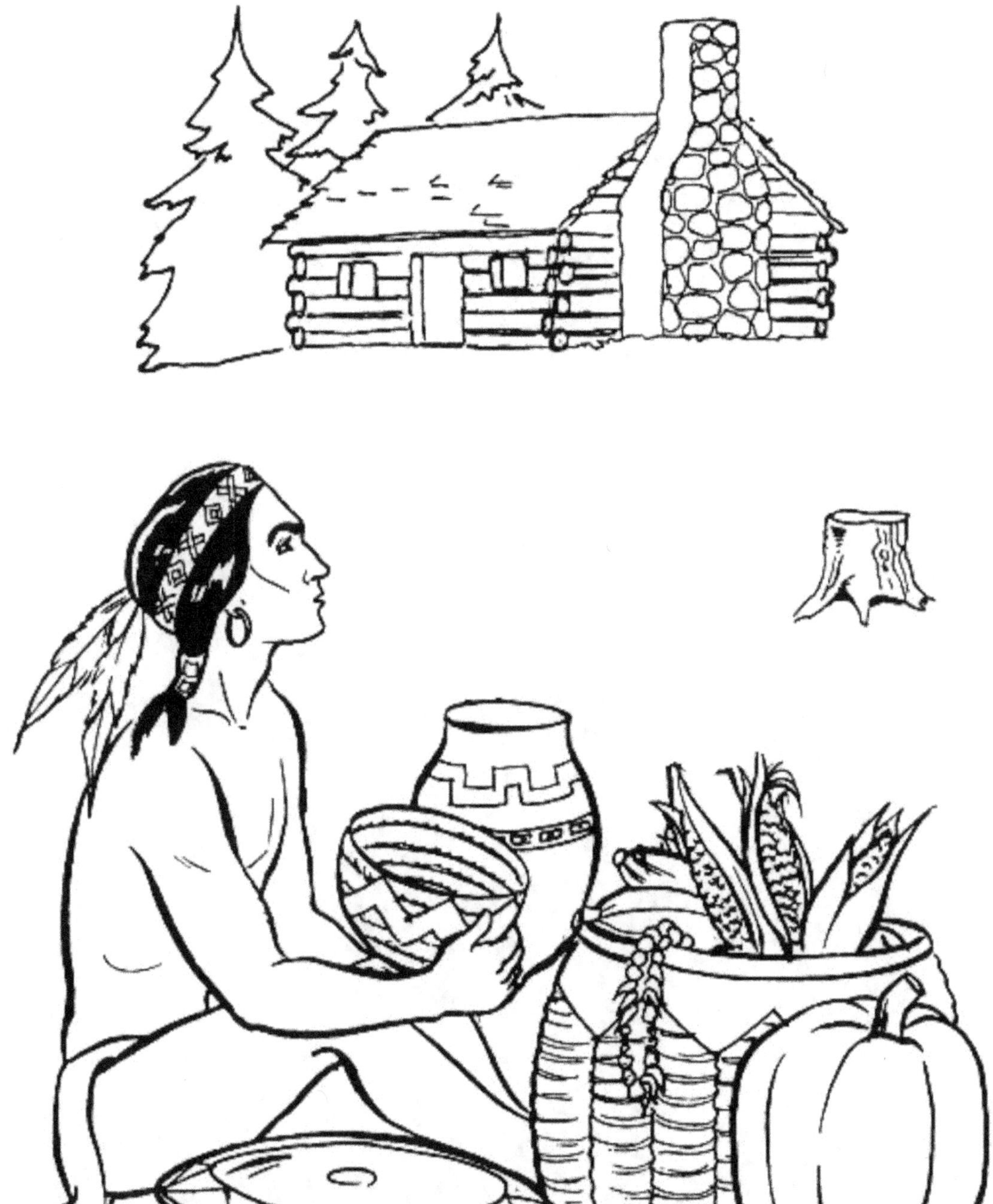

THANKSGIVING COLORING BOOK

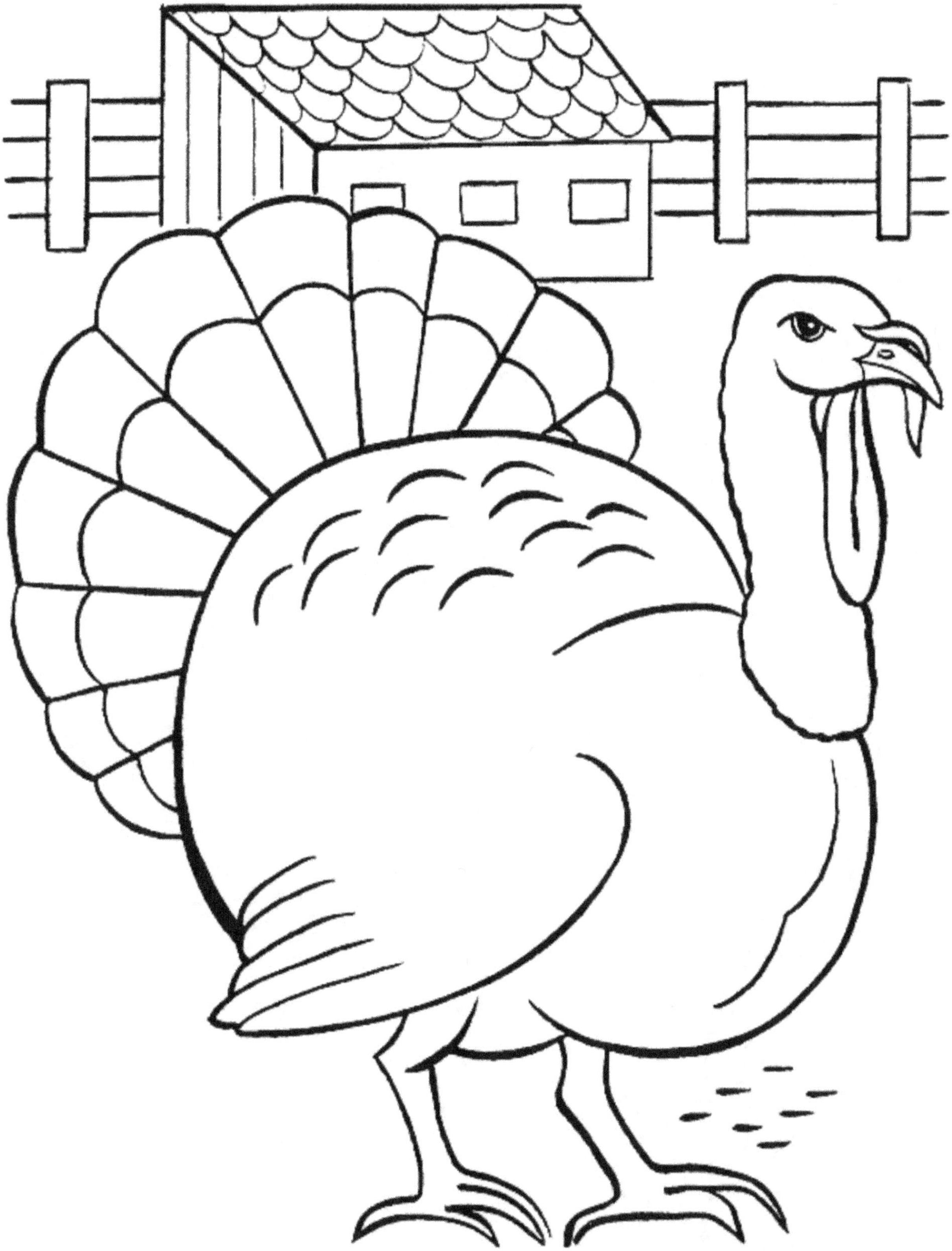

THANKSGIVING COLORING BOOK

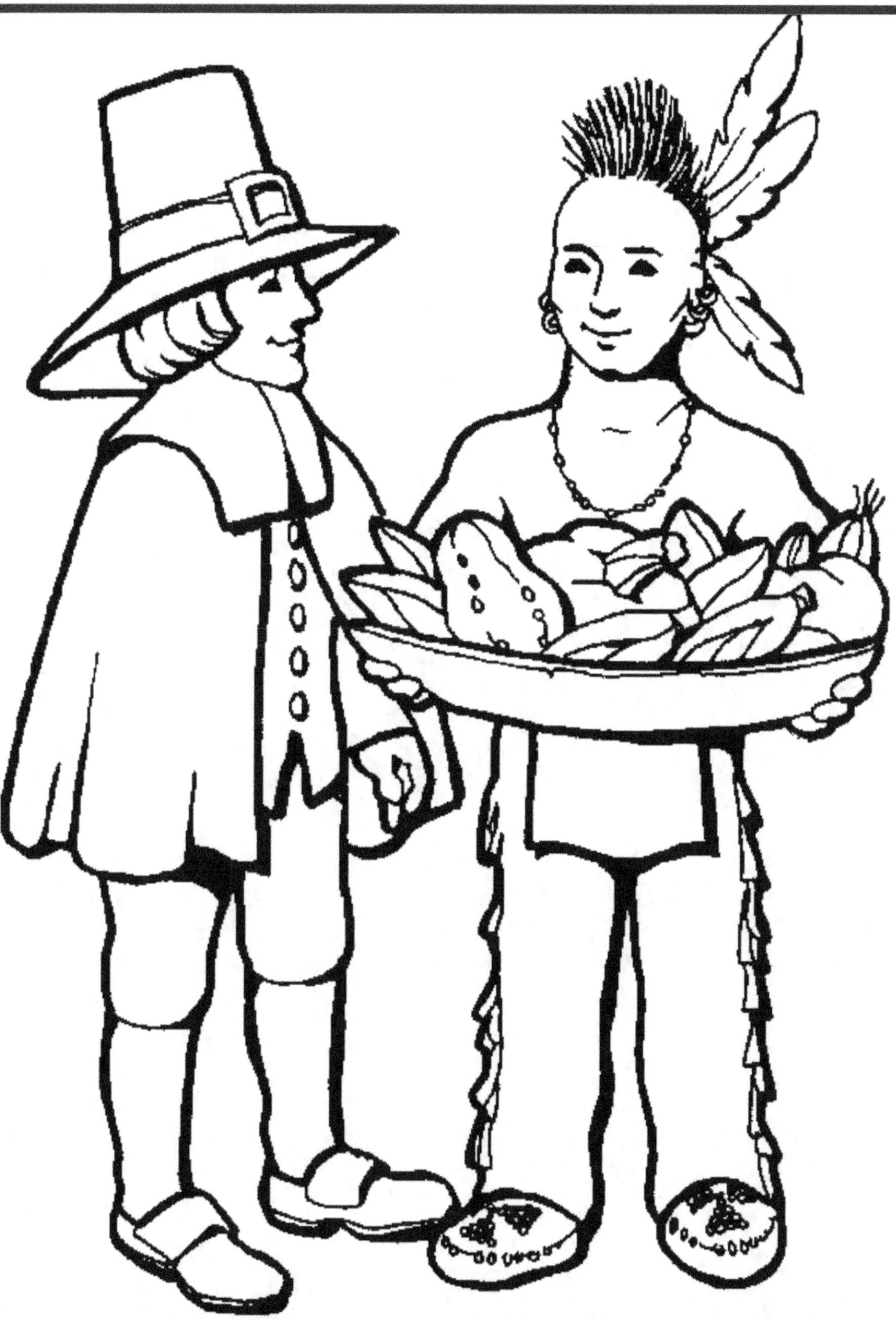

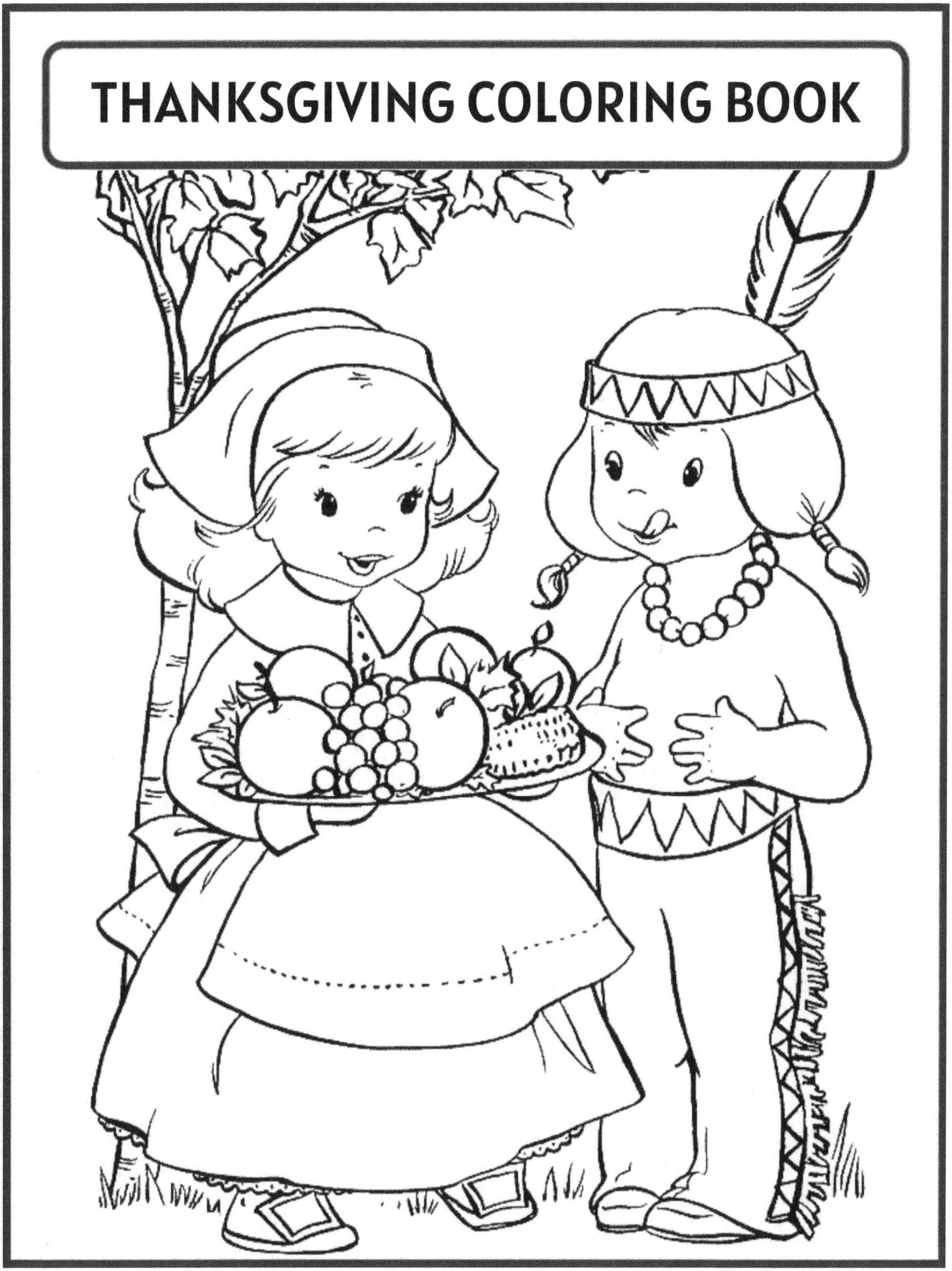
THANKSGIVING COLORING BOOK

THANKSGIVING COLORING BOOK

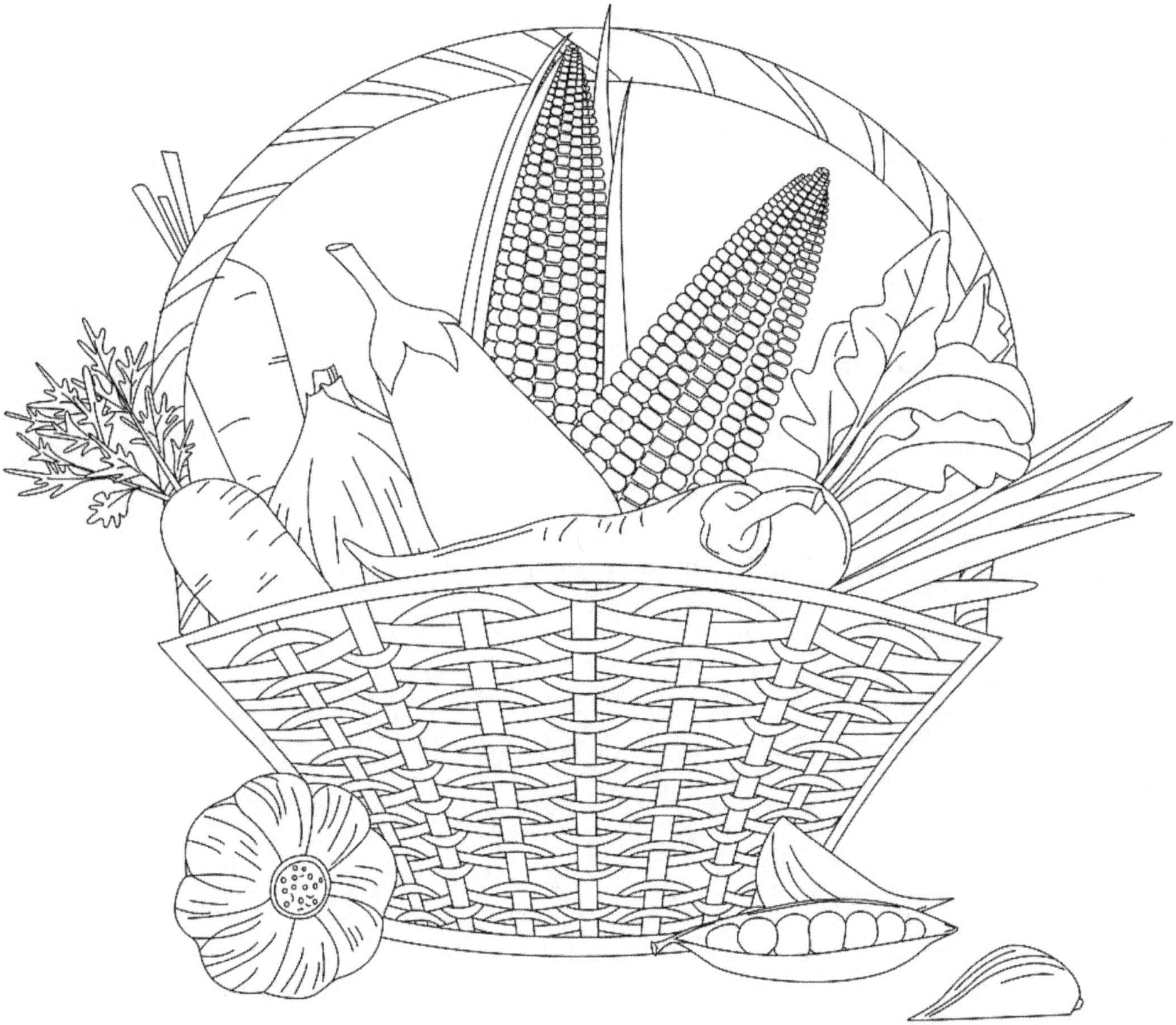

THANKSGIVING COLORING BOOK

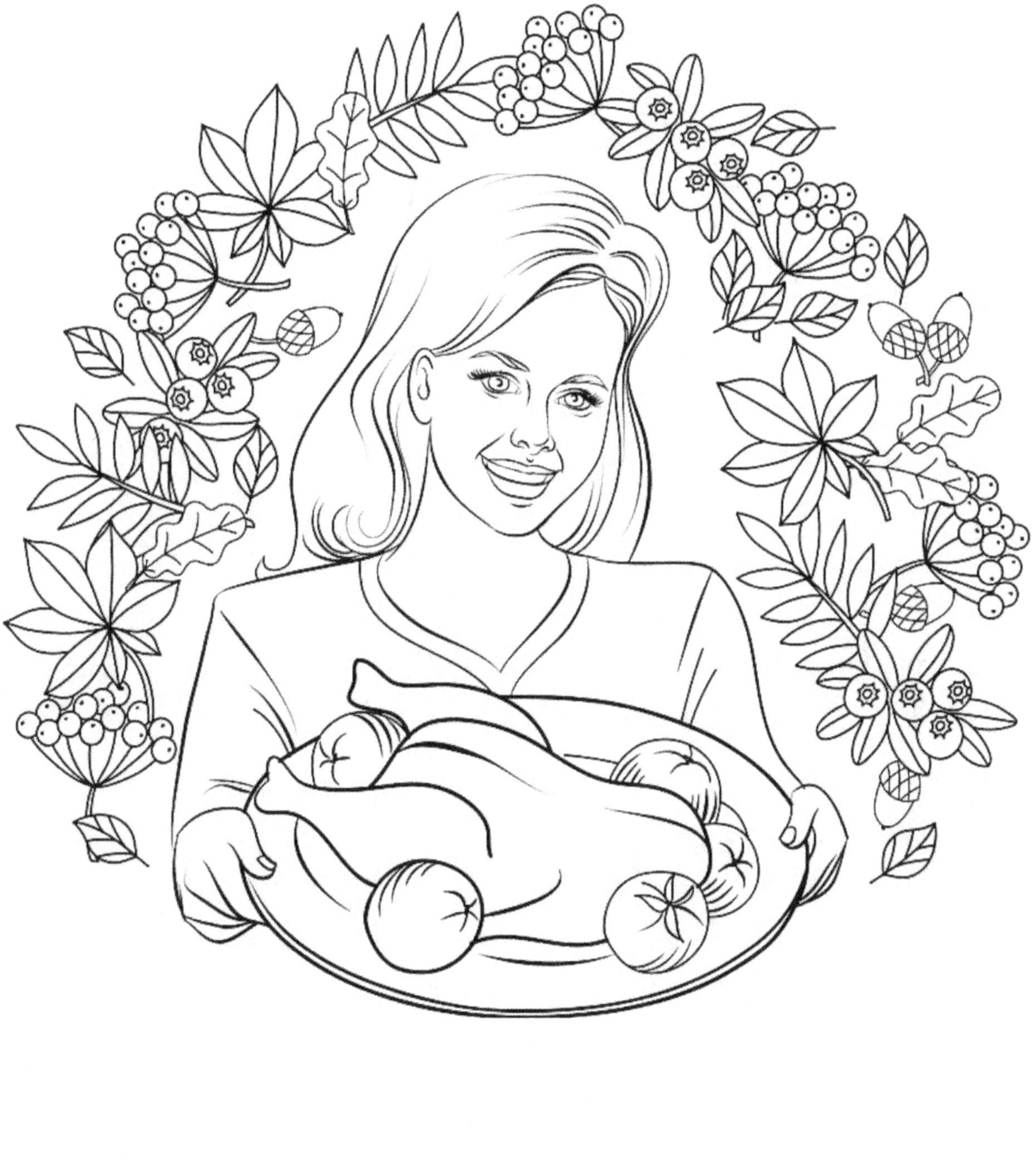

THANKSGIVING COLORING BOOK

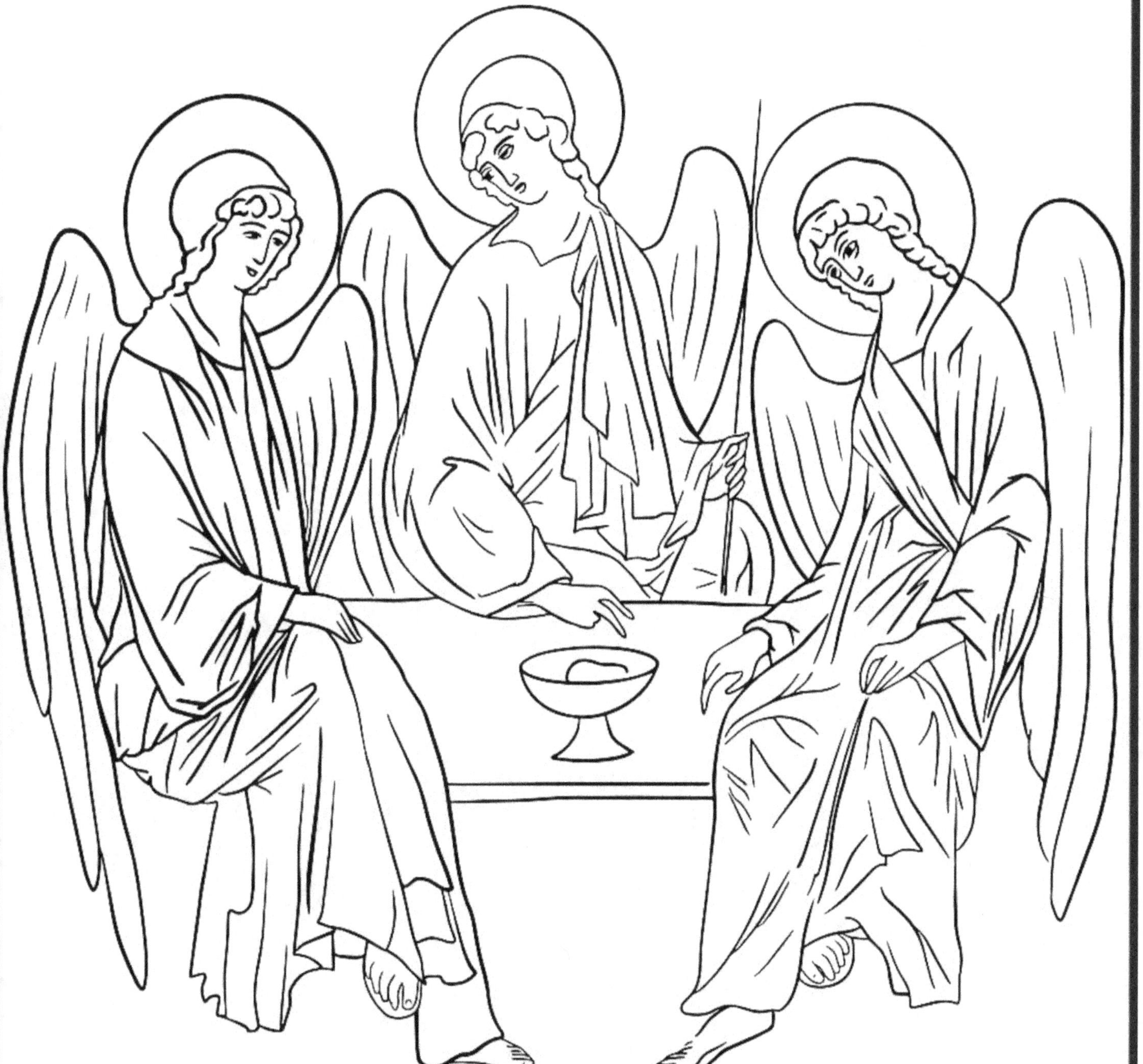

THANKSGIVING COLORING BOOK

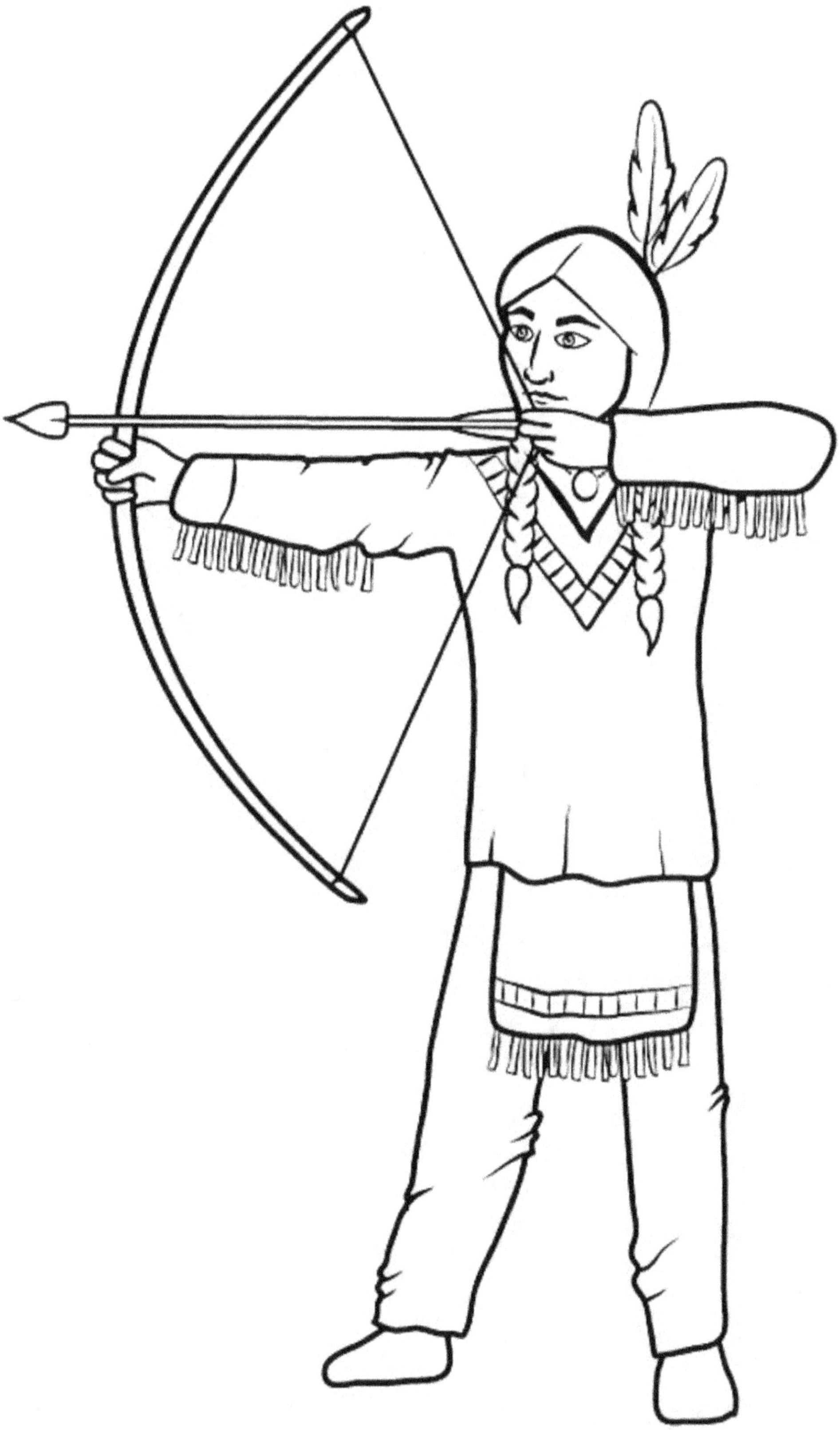

THANKSGIVING COLORING BOOK

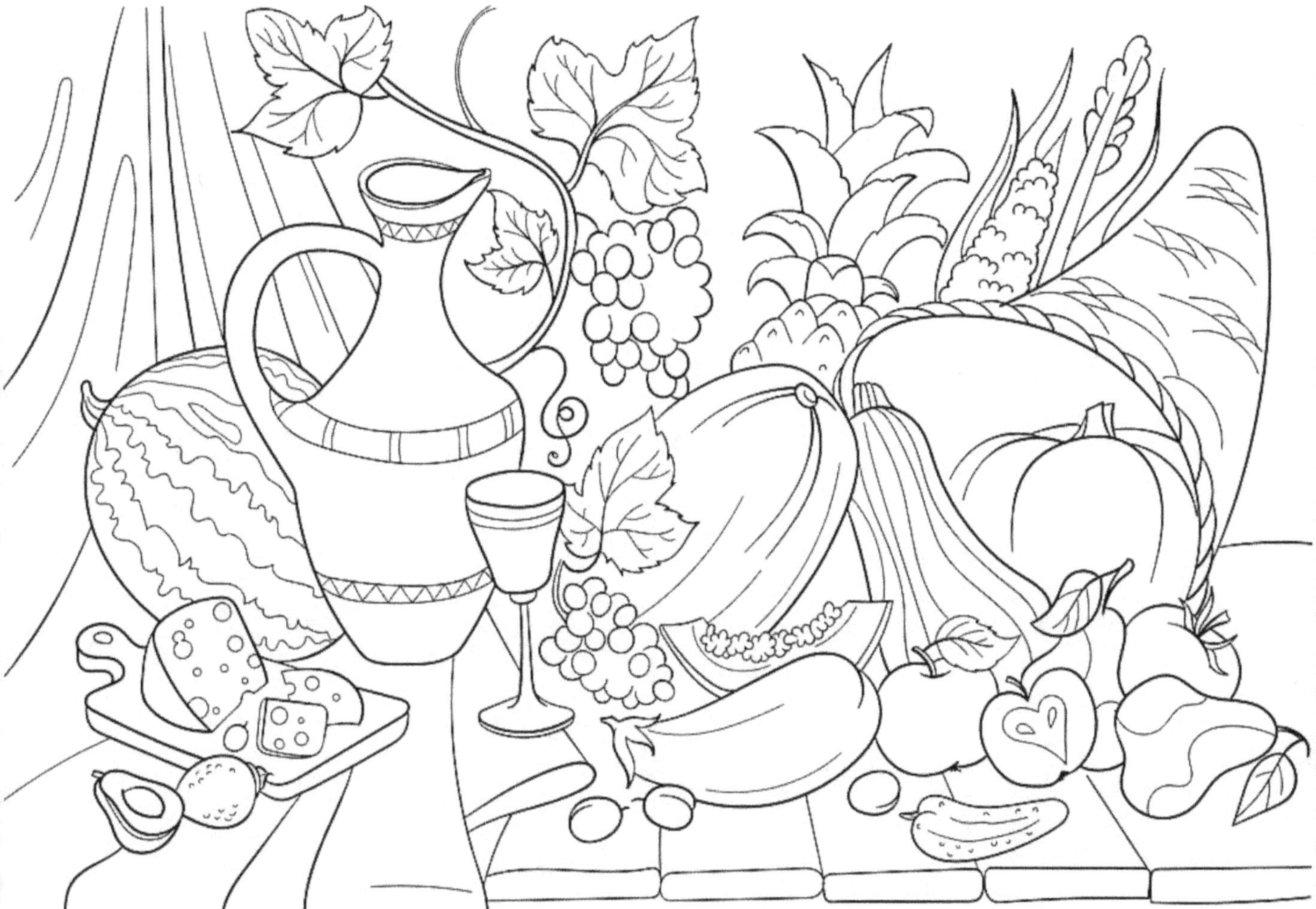

THANKSGIVING COLORING BOOK

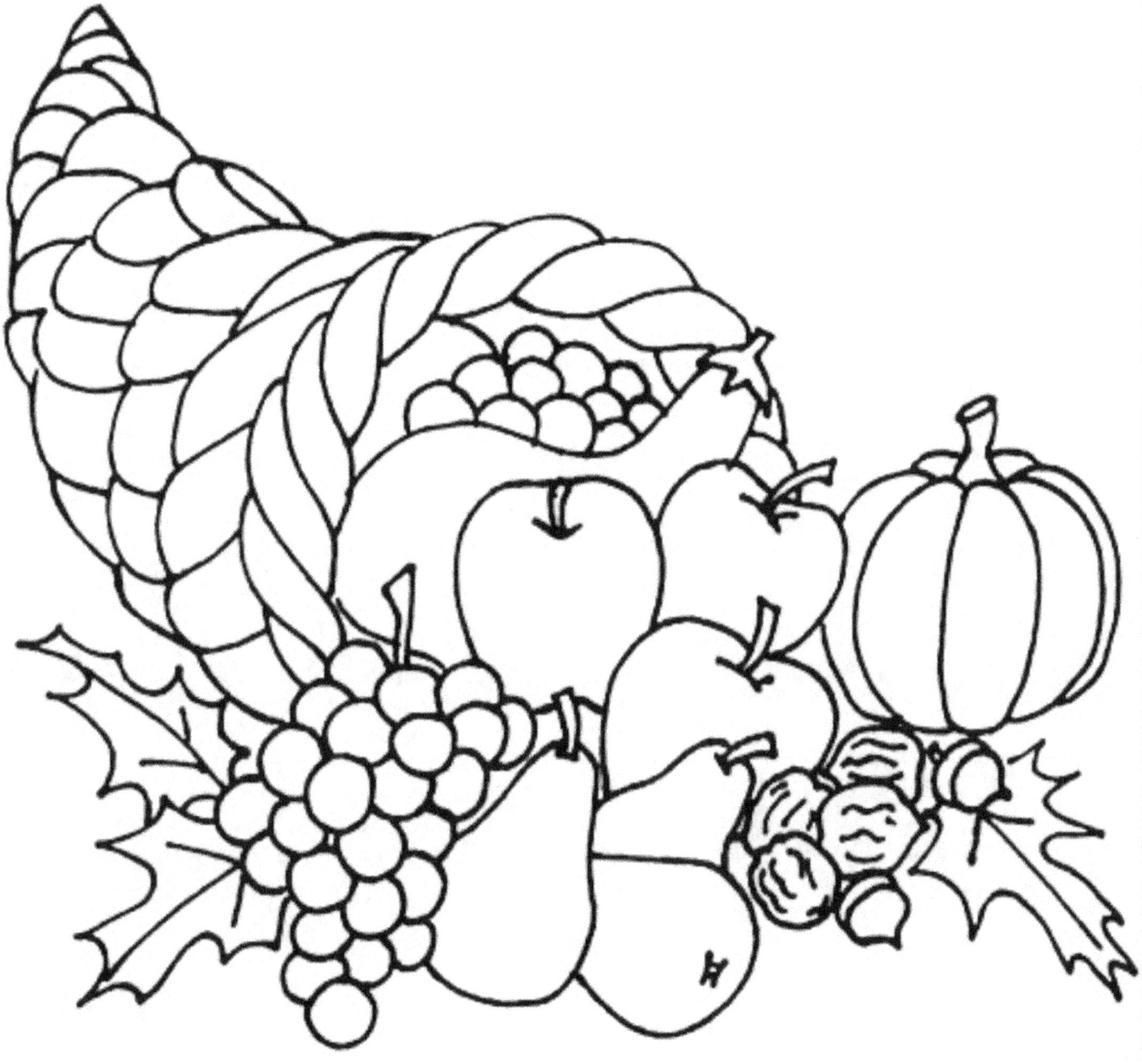

THANKSGIVING COLORING BOOK

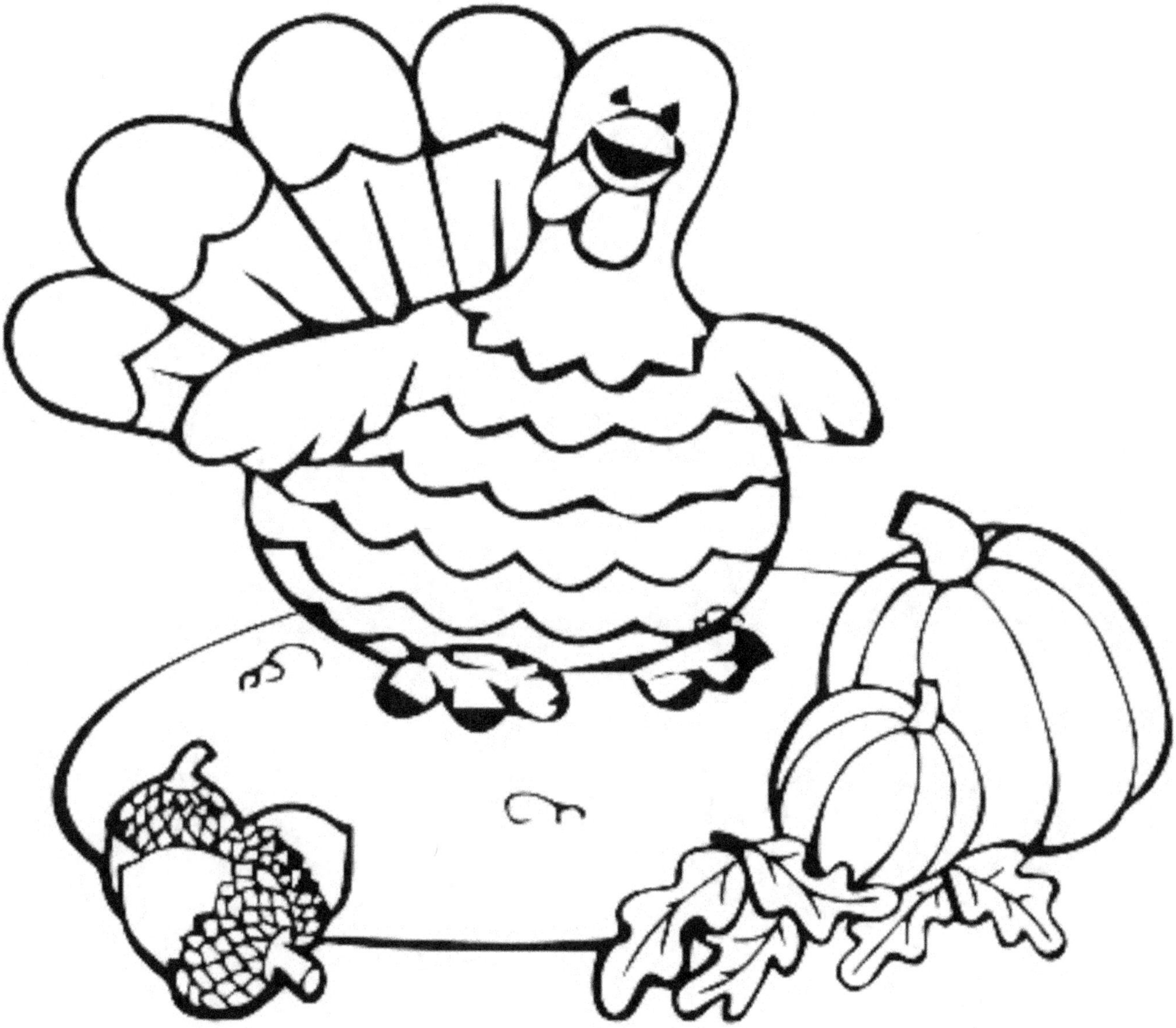

THANKSGIVING COLORING BOOK

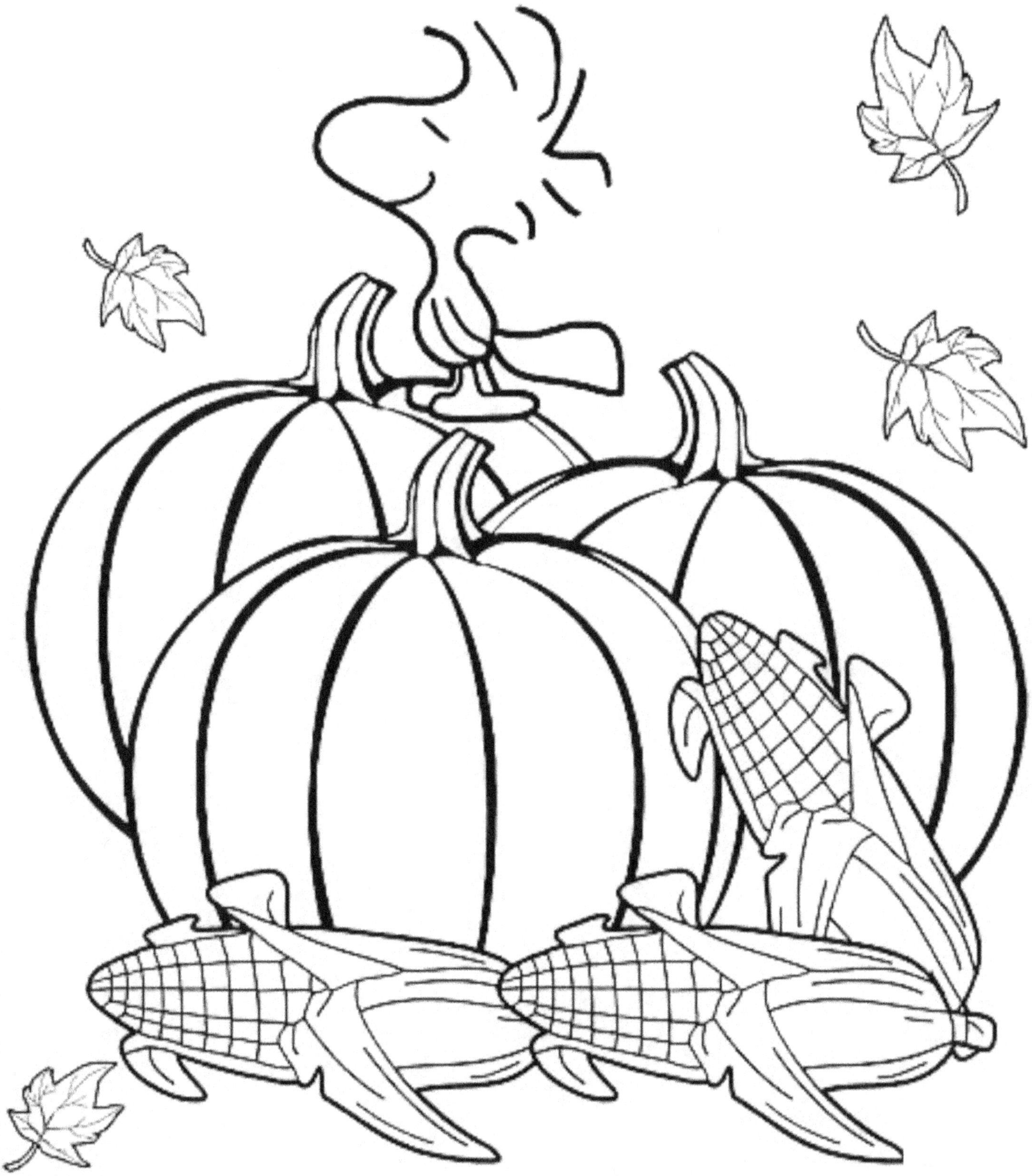

THANKSGIVING COLORING BOOK

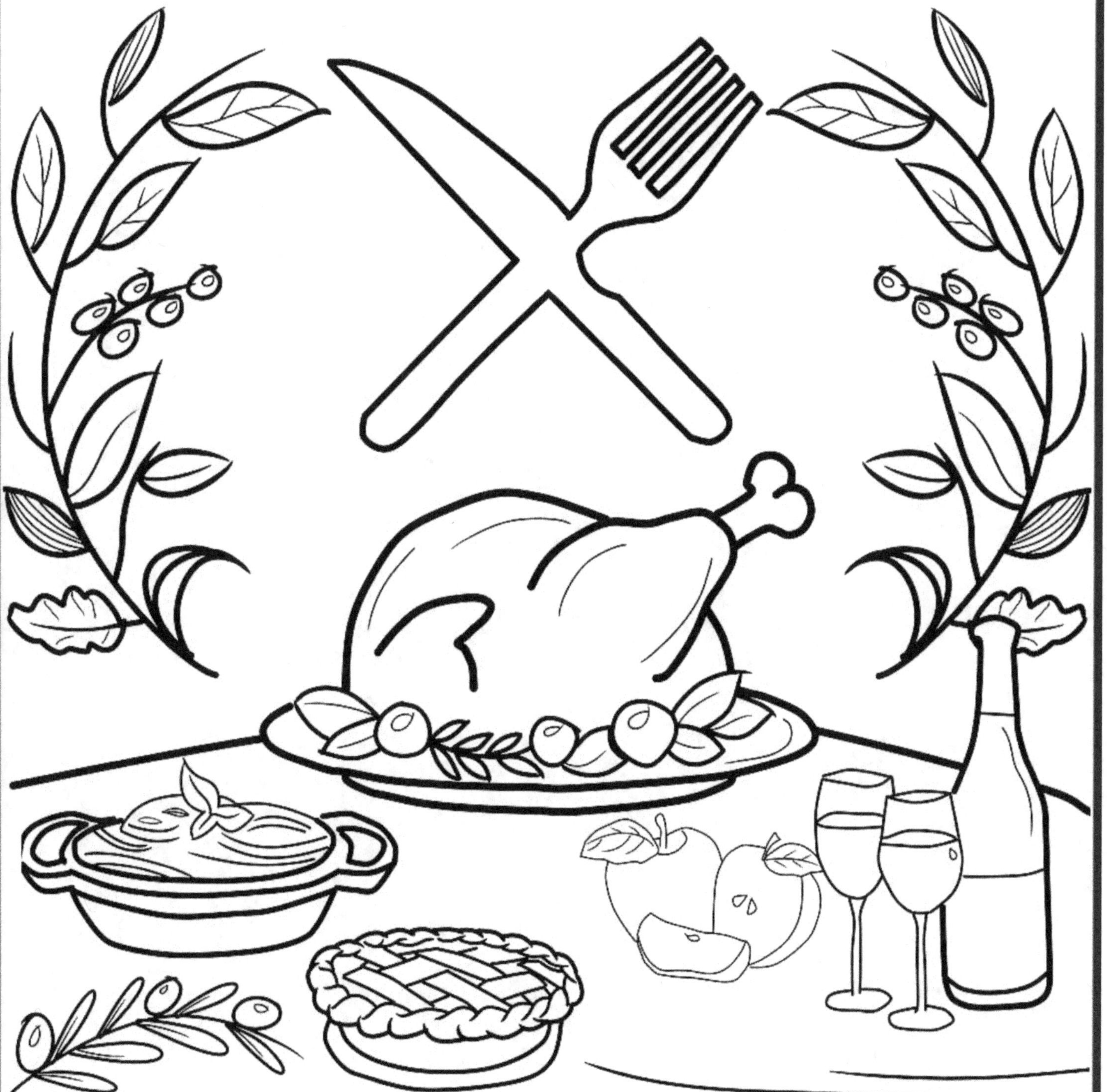

THANKSGIVING COLORING BOOK

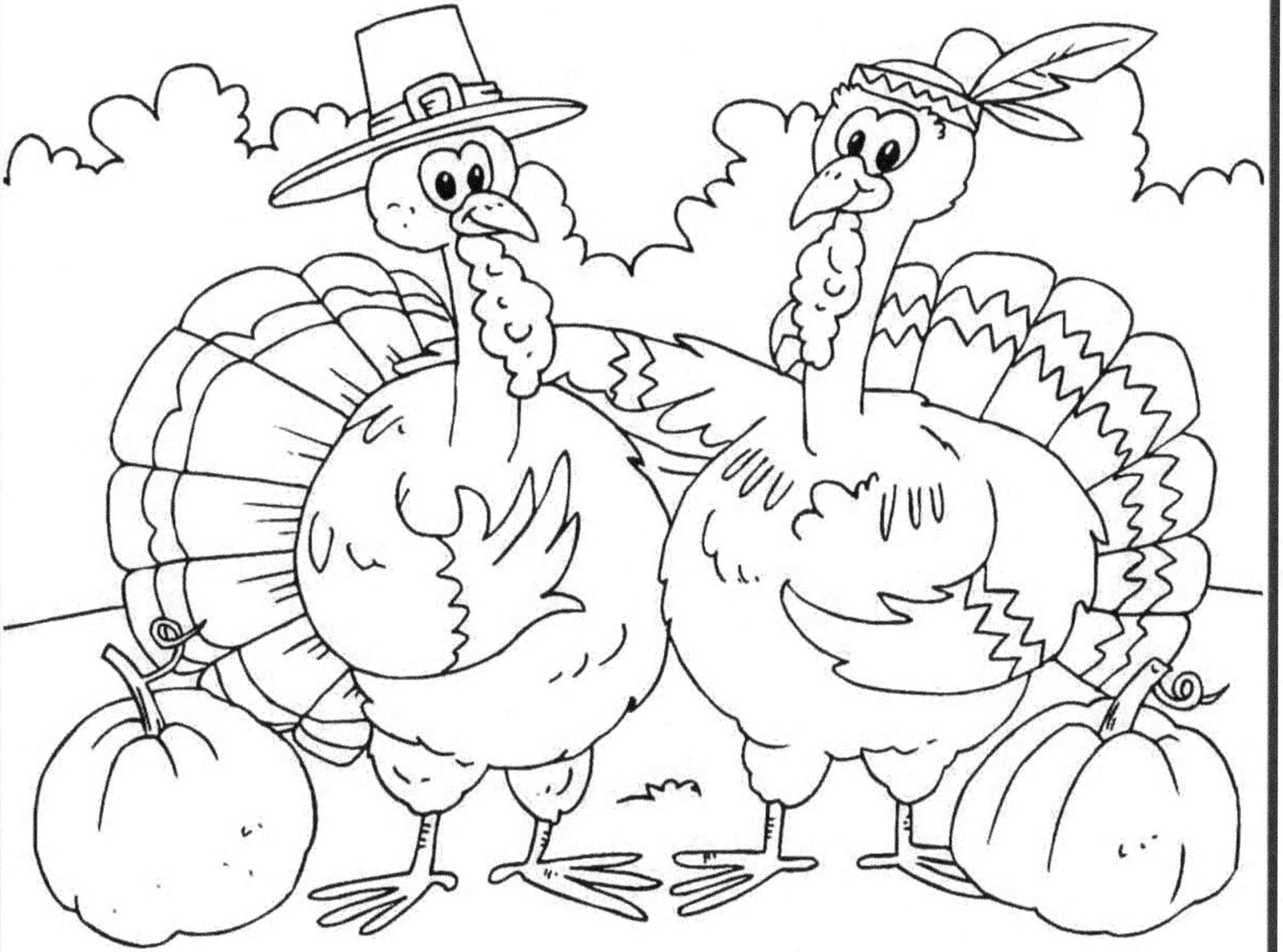

THANKSGIVING COLORING BOOK

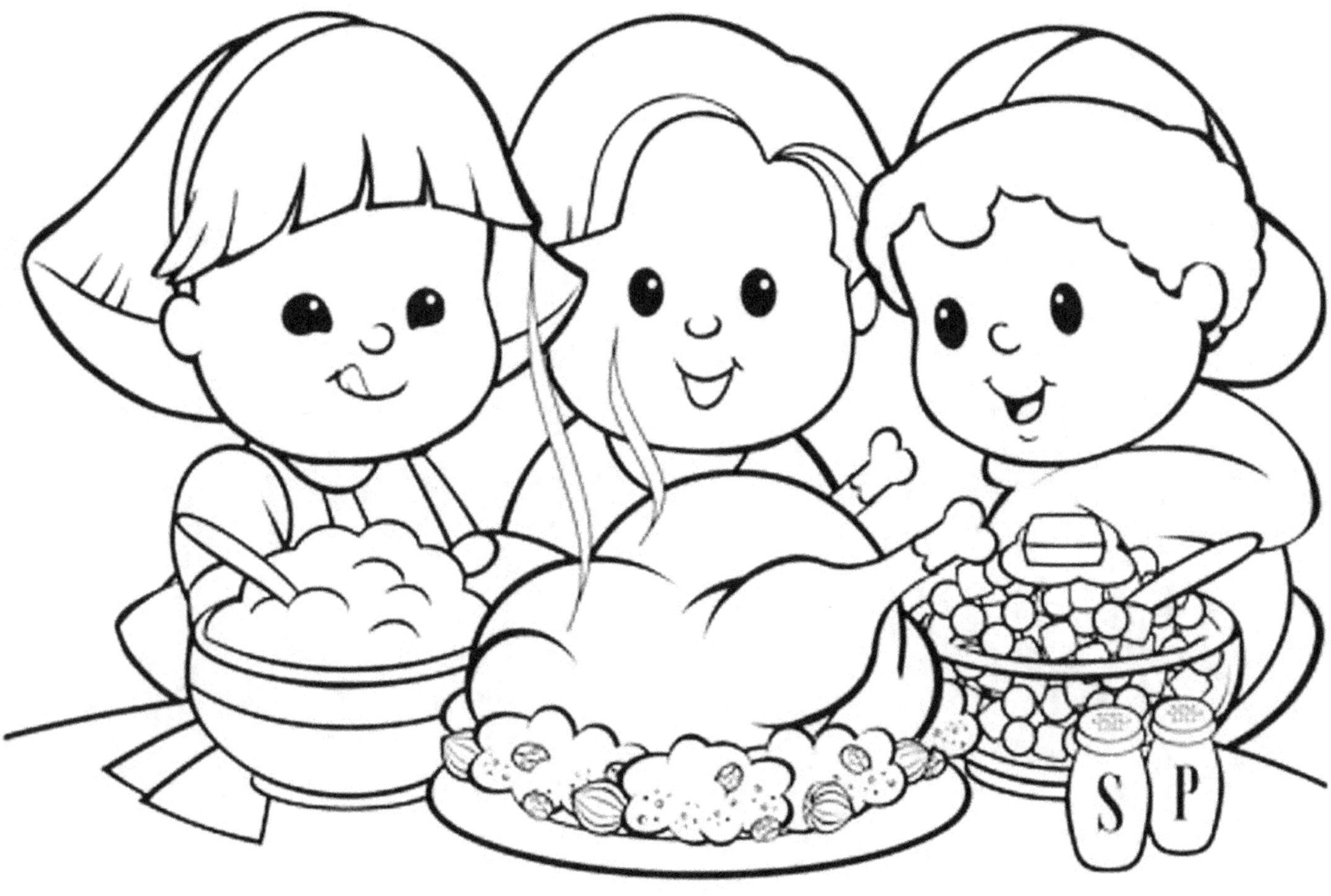

THANKSGIVING COLORING BOOK

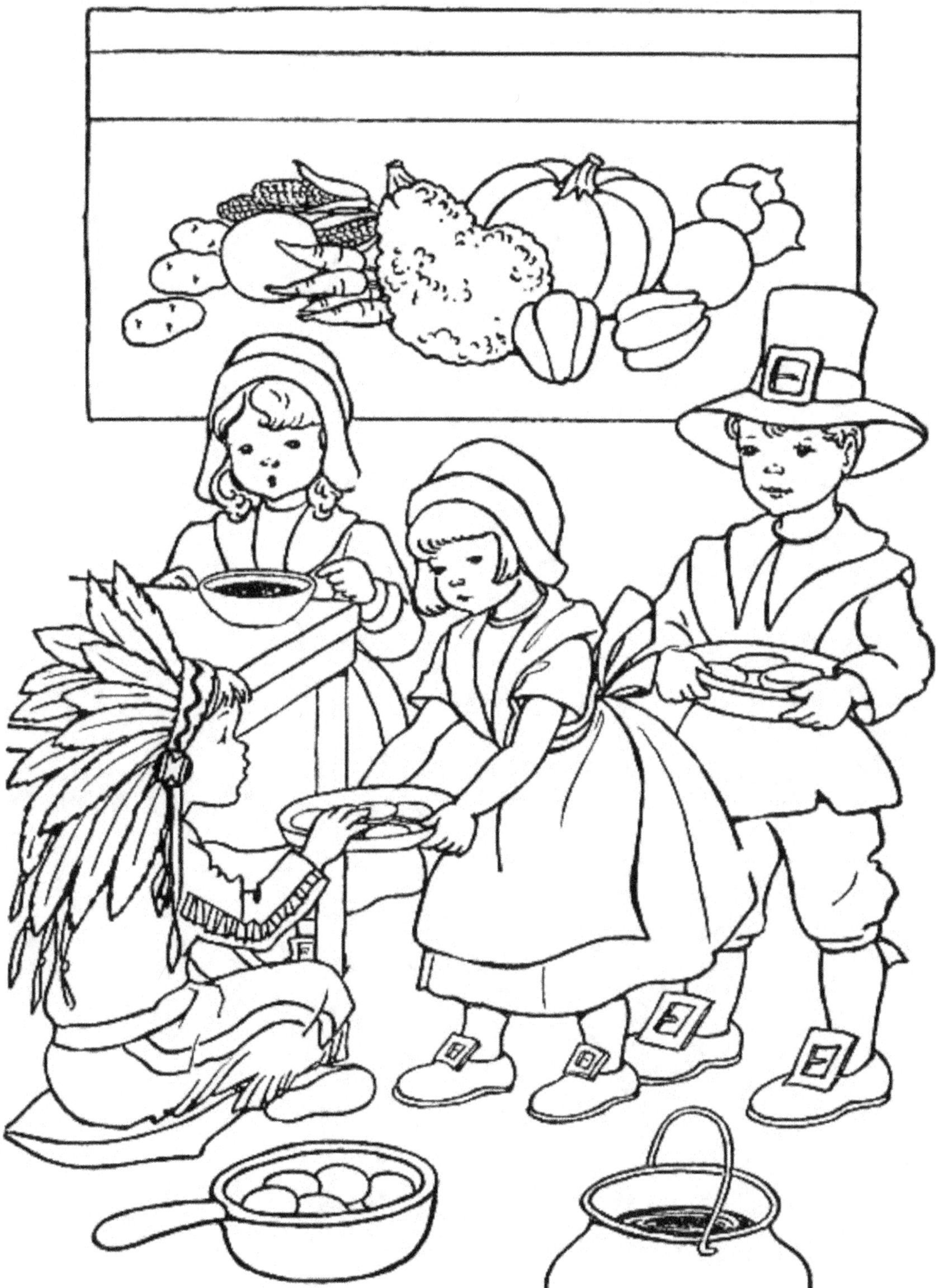

THANKSGIVING COLORING BOOK

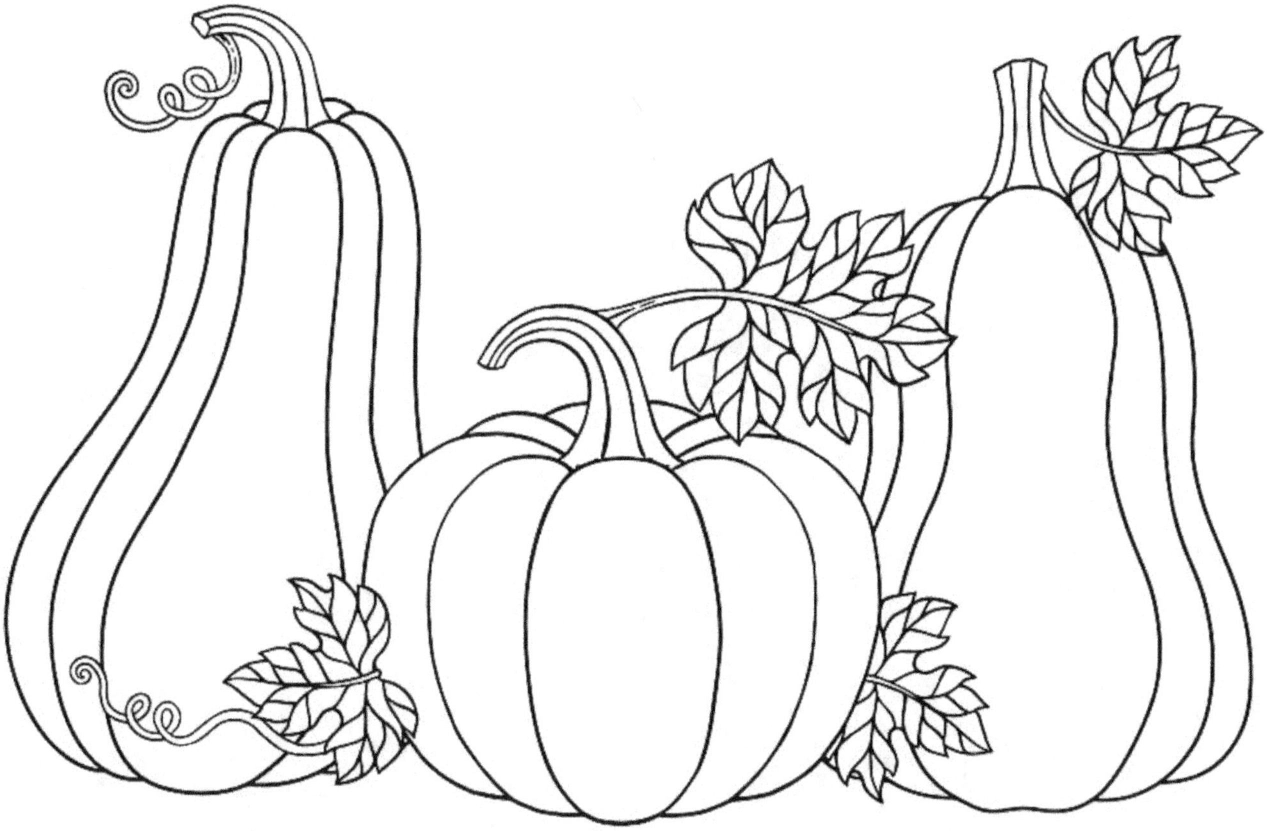

THANKSGIVING COLORING BOOK

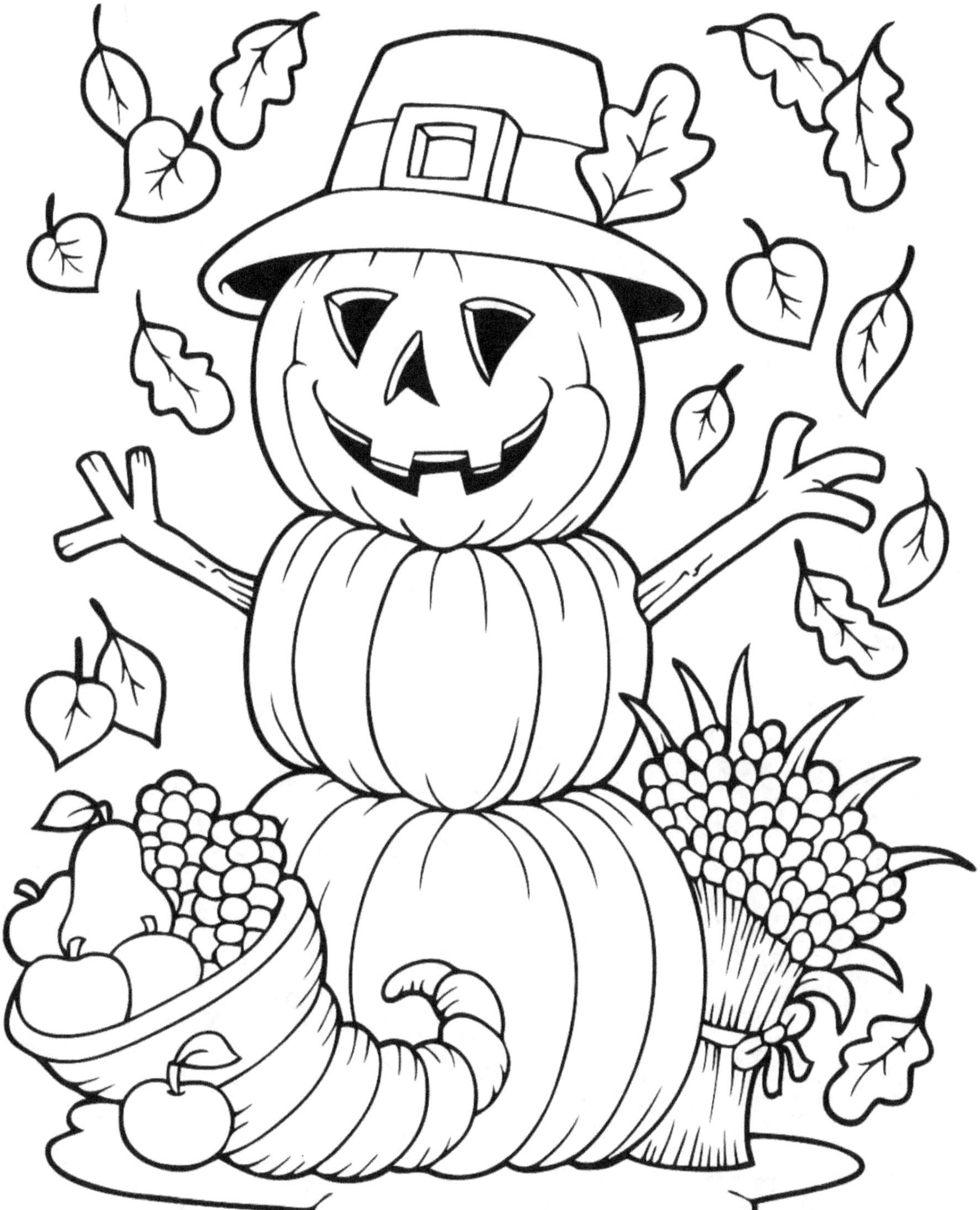

THANKSGIVING COLORING BOOK

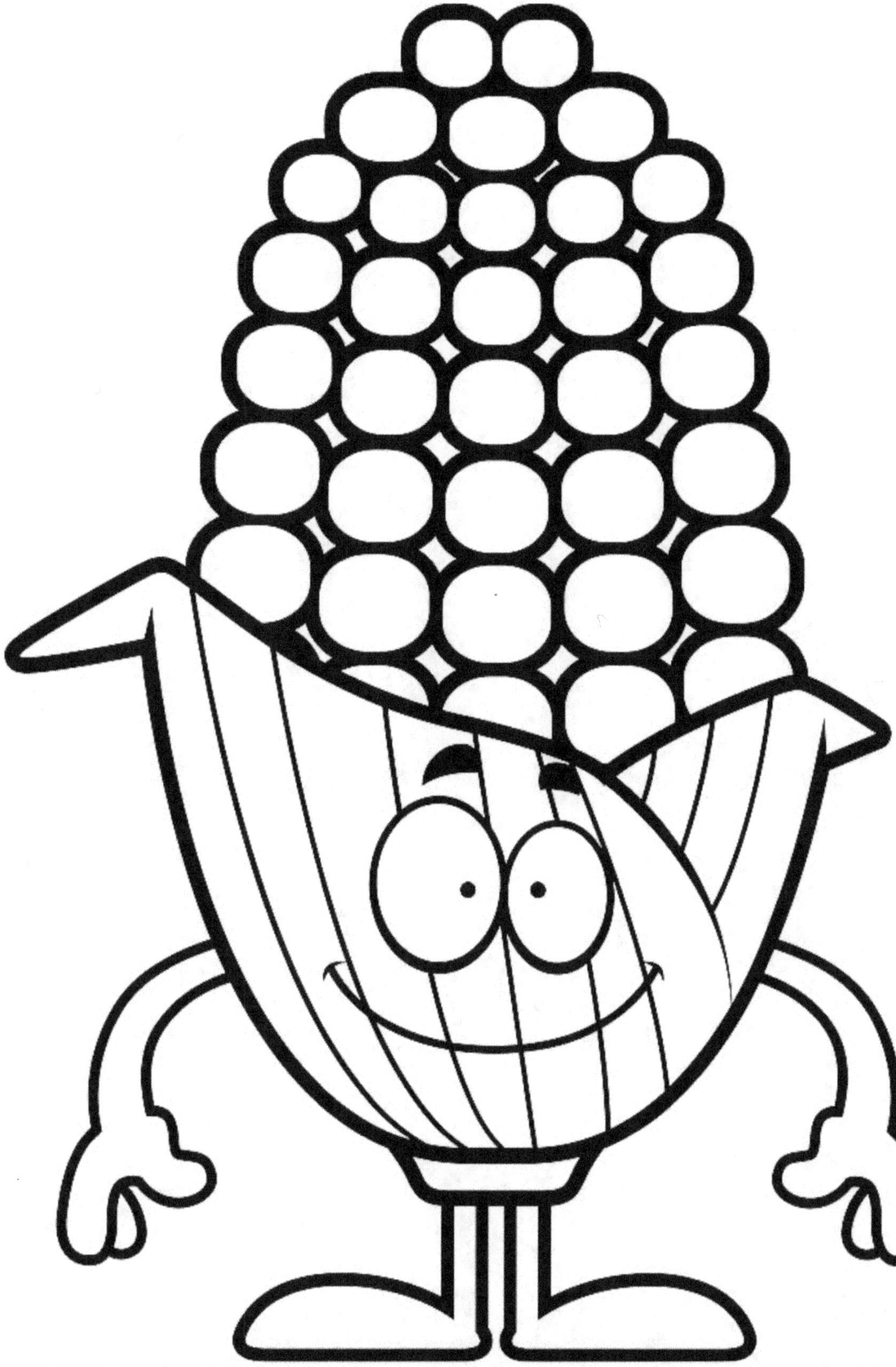

THANKSGIVING COLORING BOOK

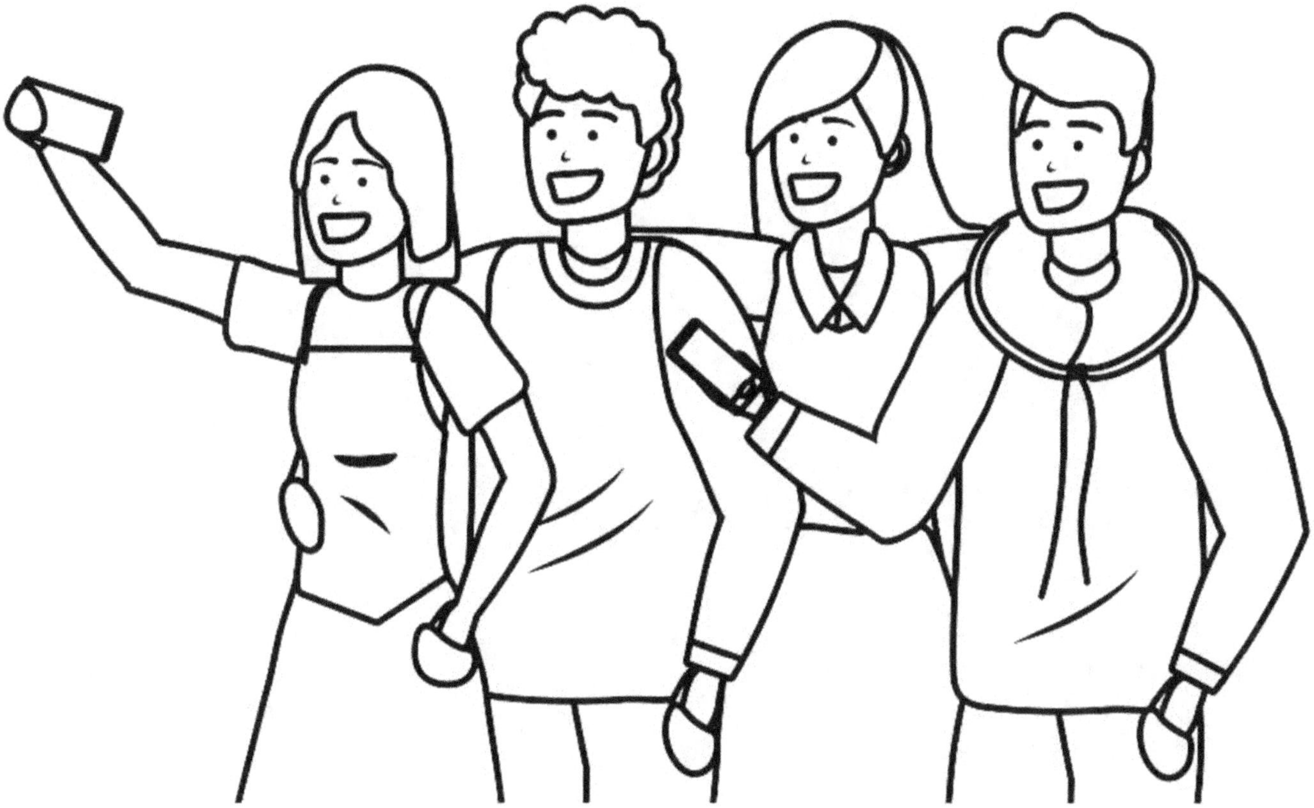

THANKSGIVING COLORING BOOK

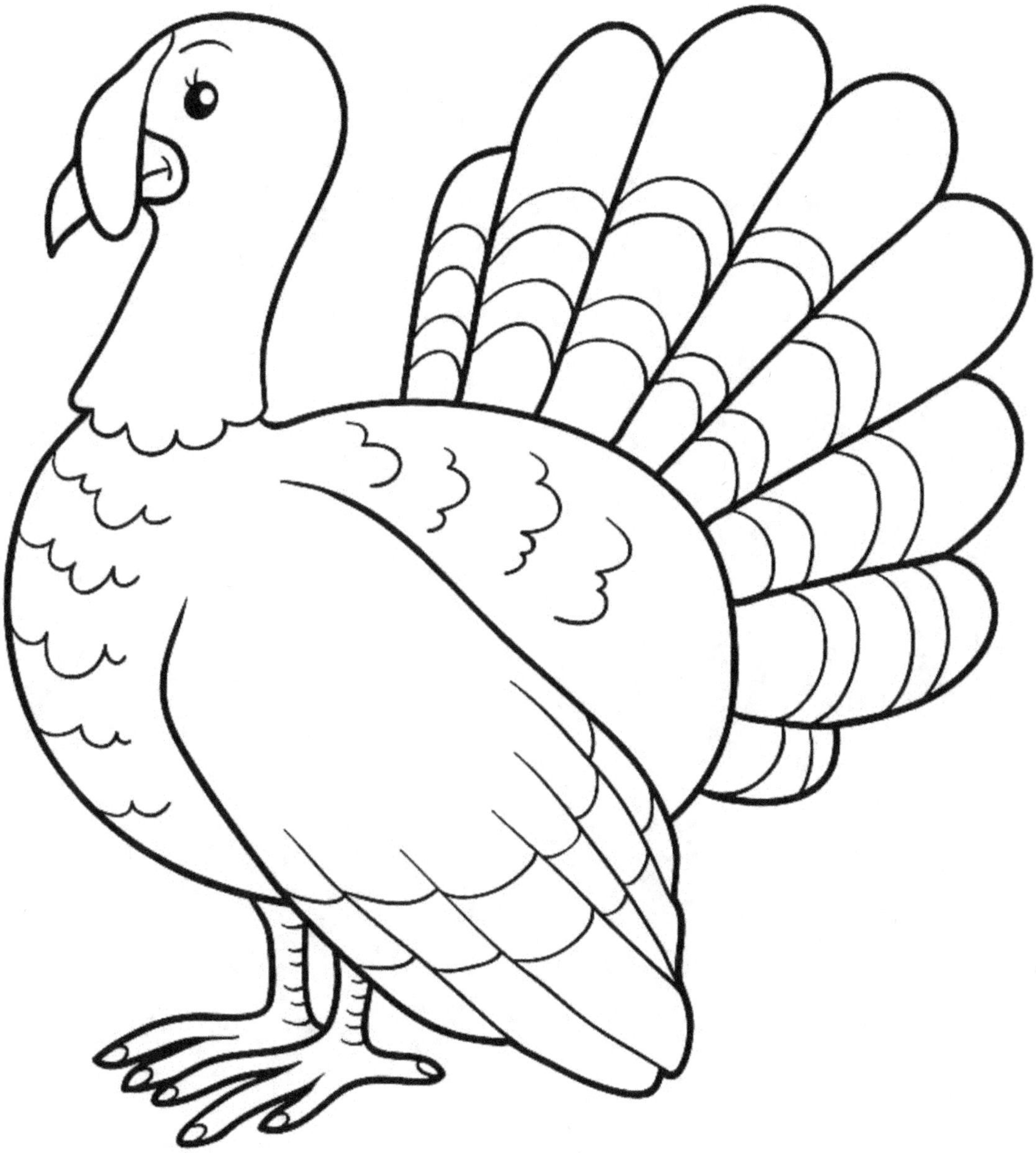

THANKSGIVING COLORING BOOK

THANKSGIVING COLORING BOOK

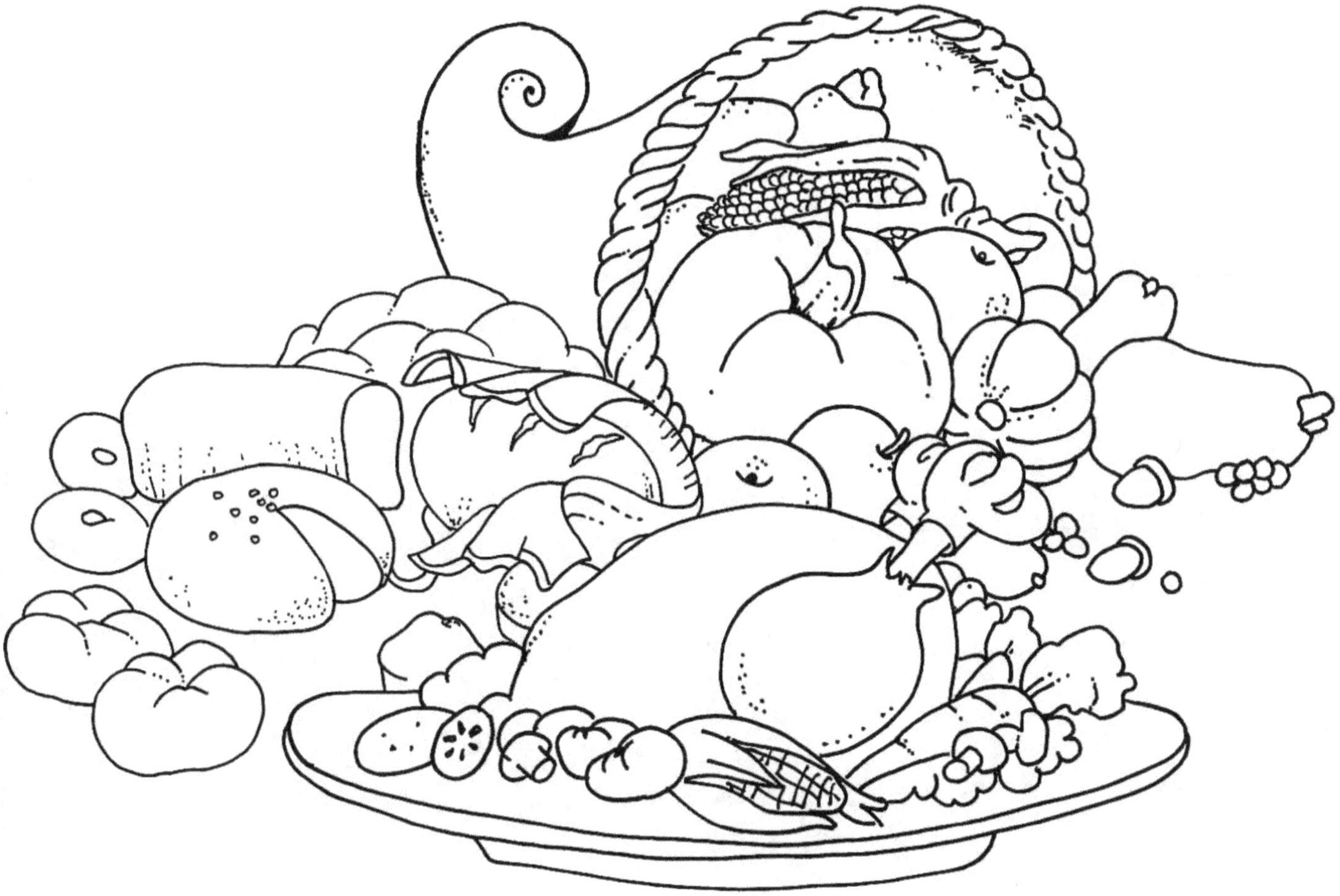

THANKSGIVING COLORING BOOK

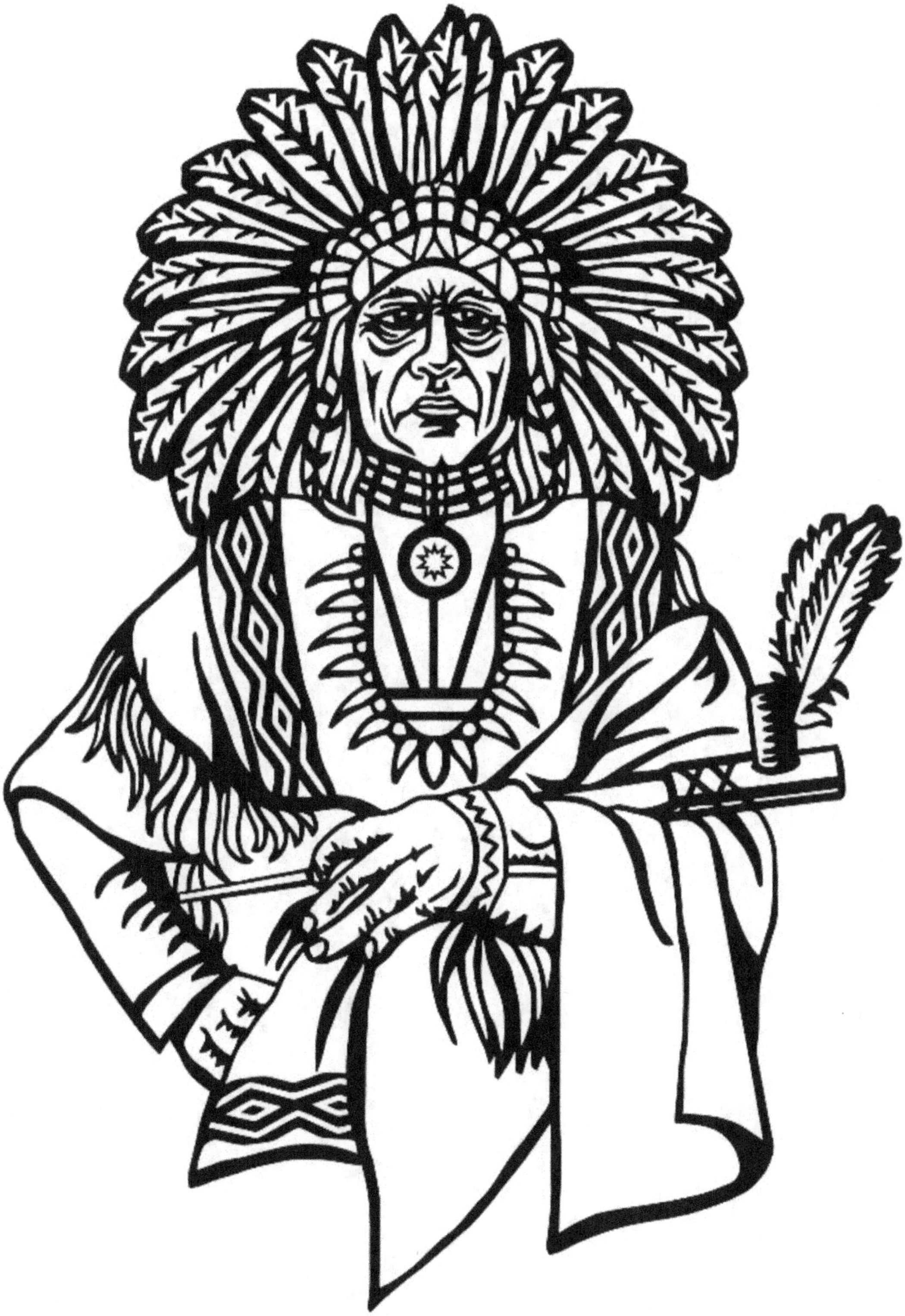

THANKSGIVING COLORING BOOK

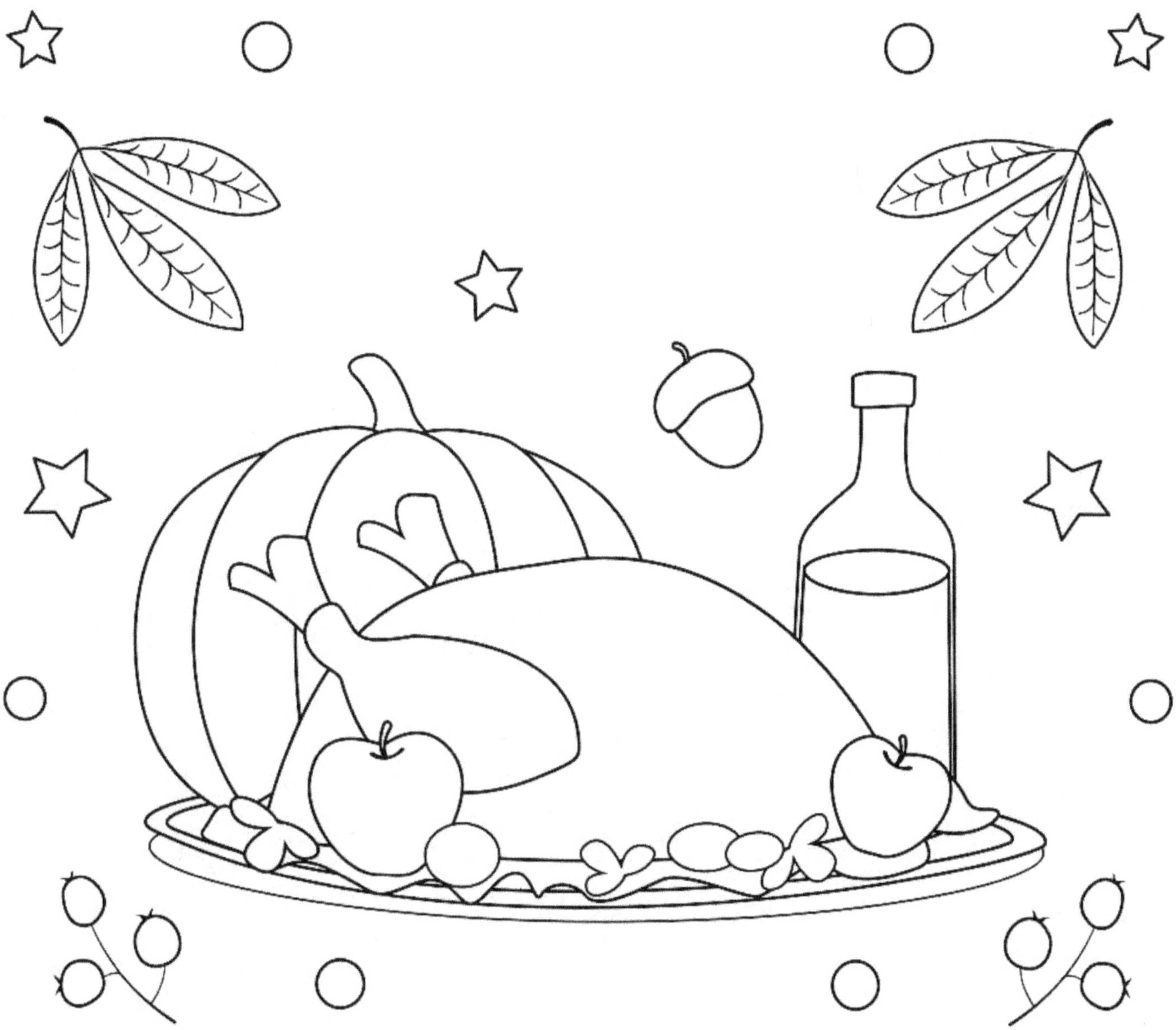

THANKSGIVING COLORING BOOK

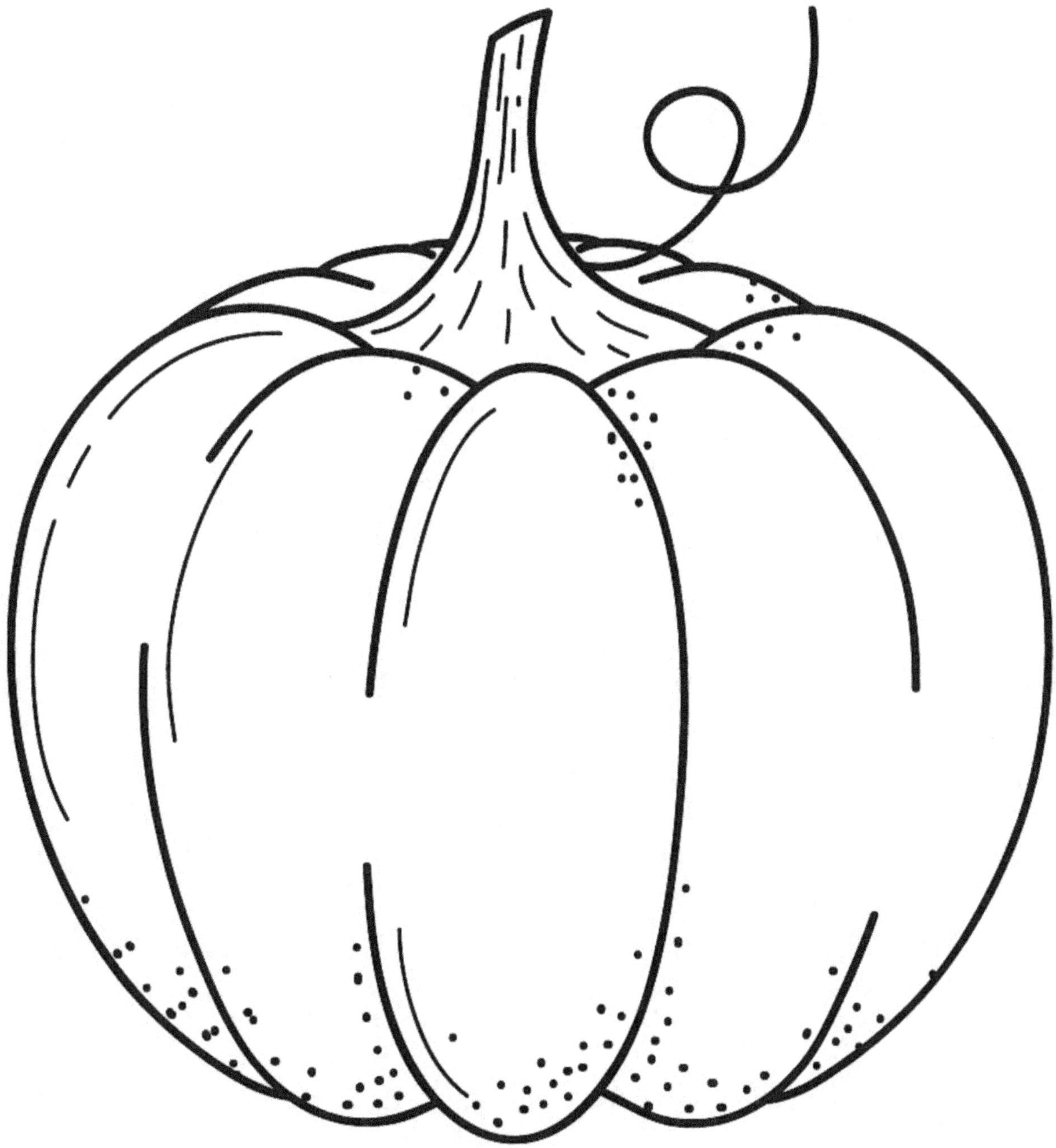

THANKSGIVING COLORING BOOK

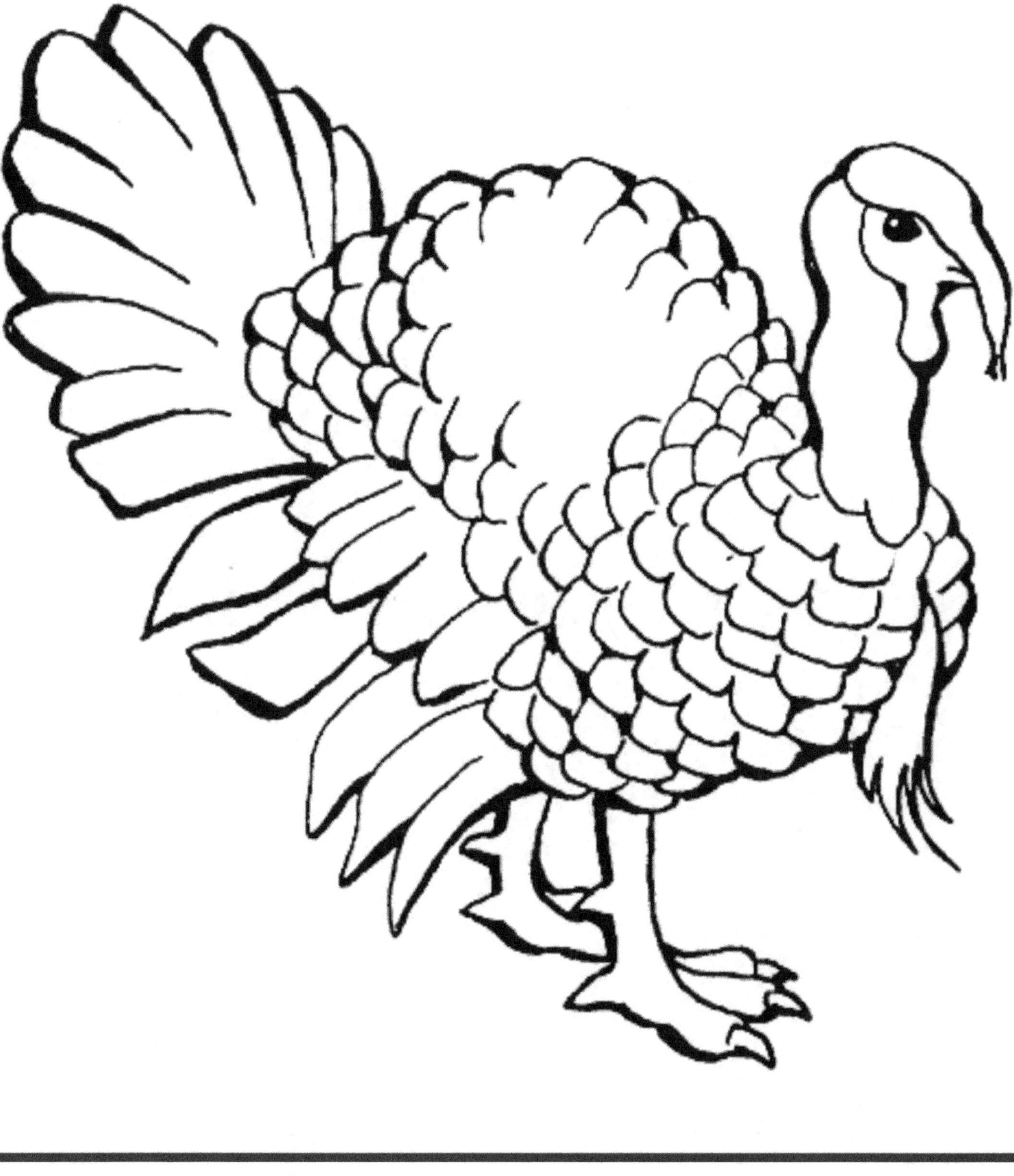

THANKSGIVING COLORING BOOK

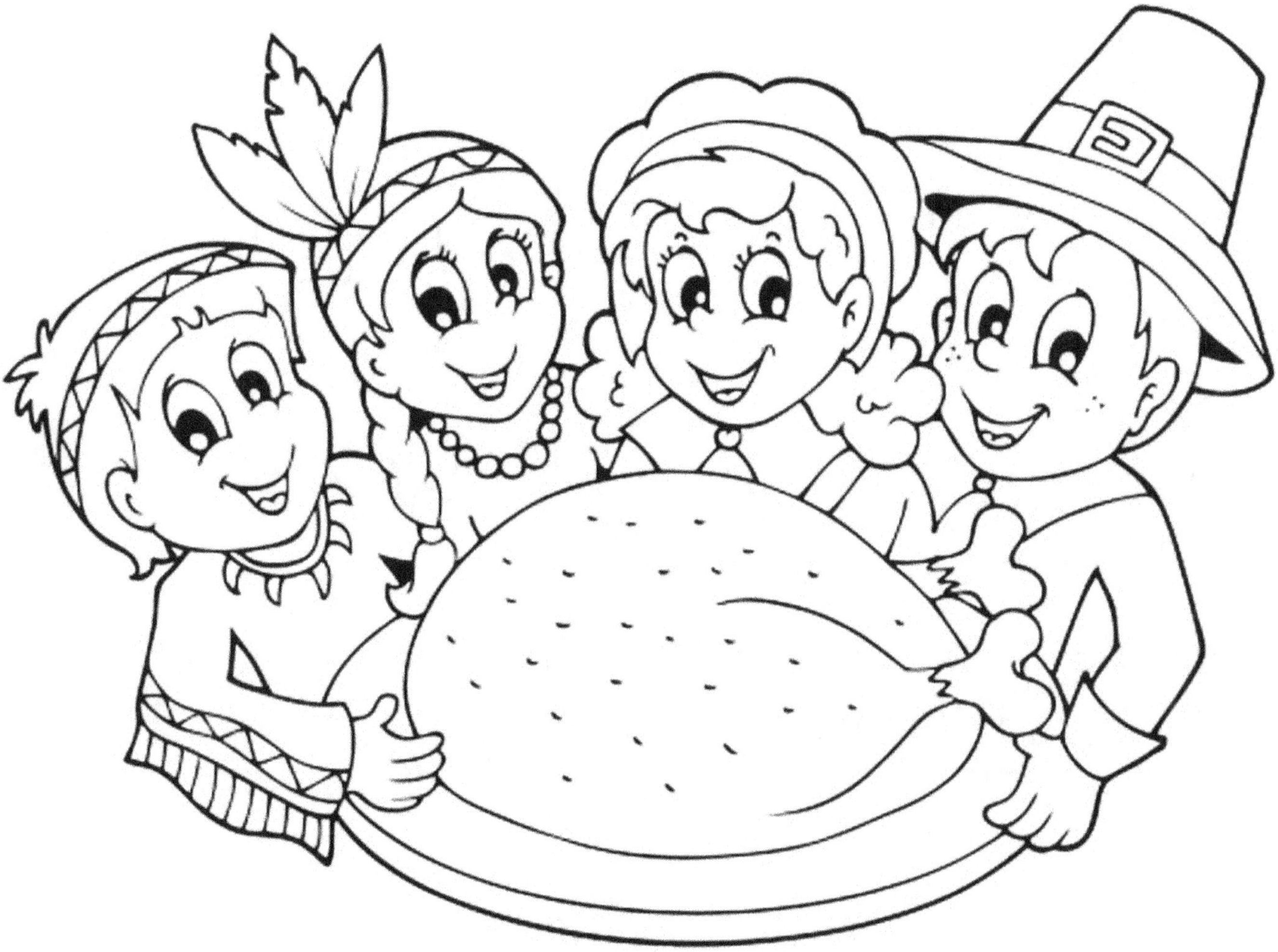

THANKSGIVING COLORING BOOK

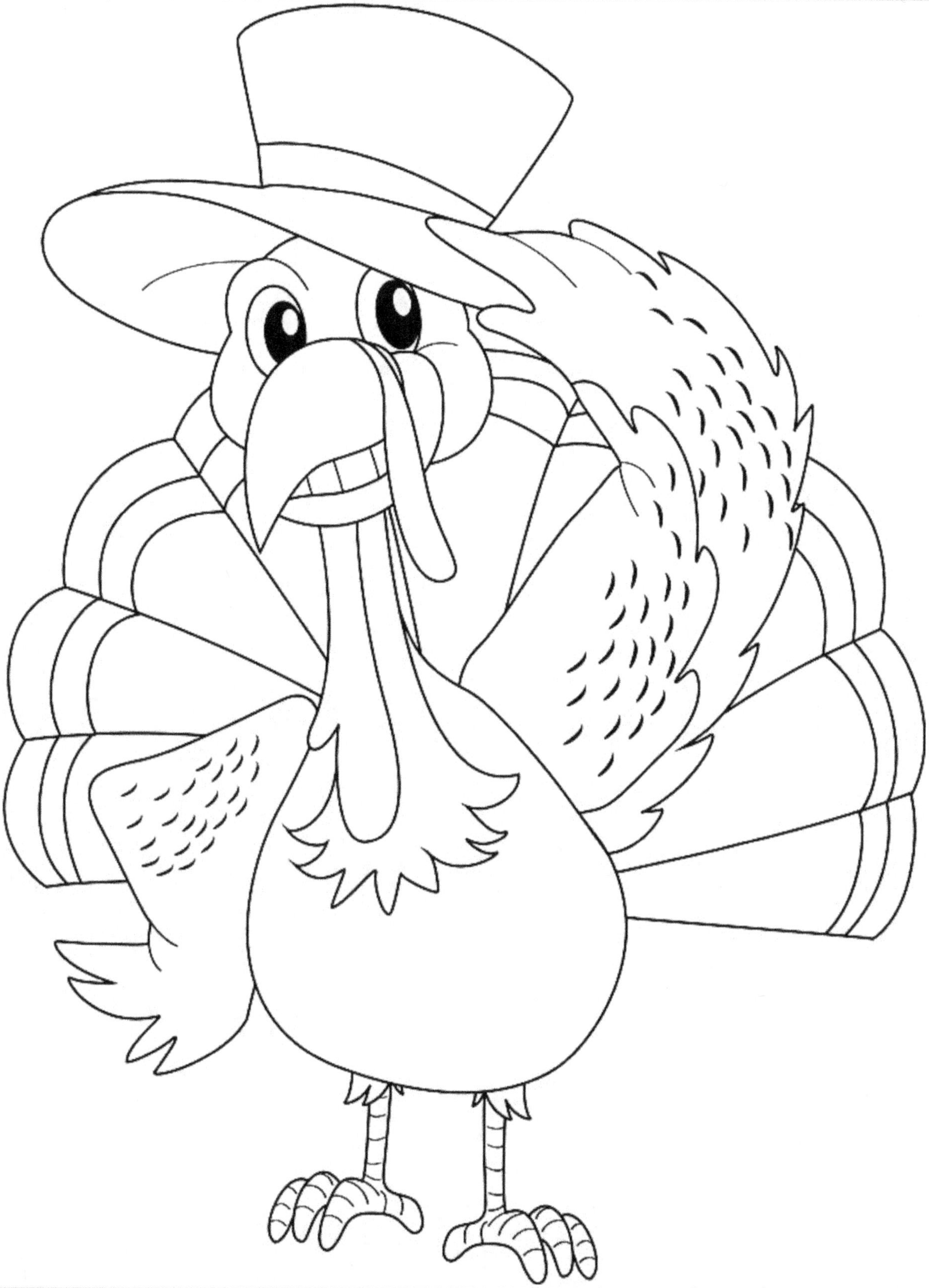

THANKSGIVING COLORING BOOK

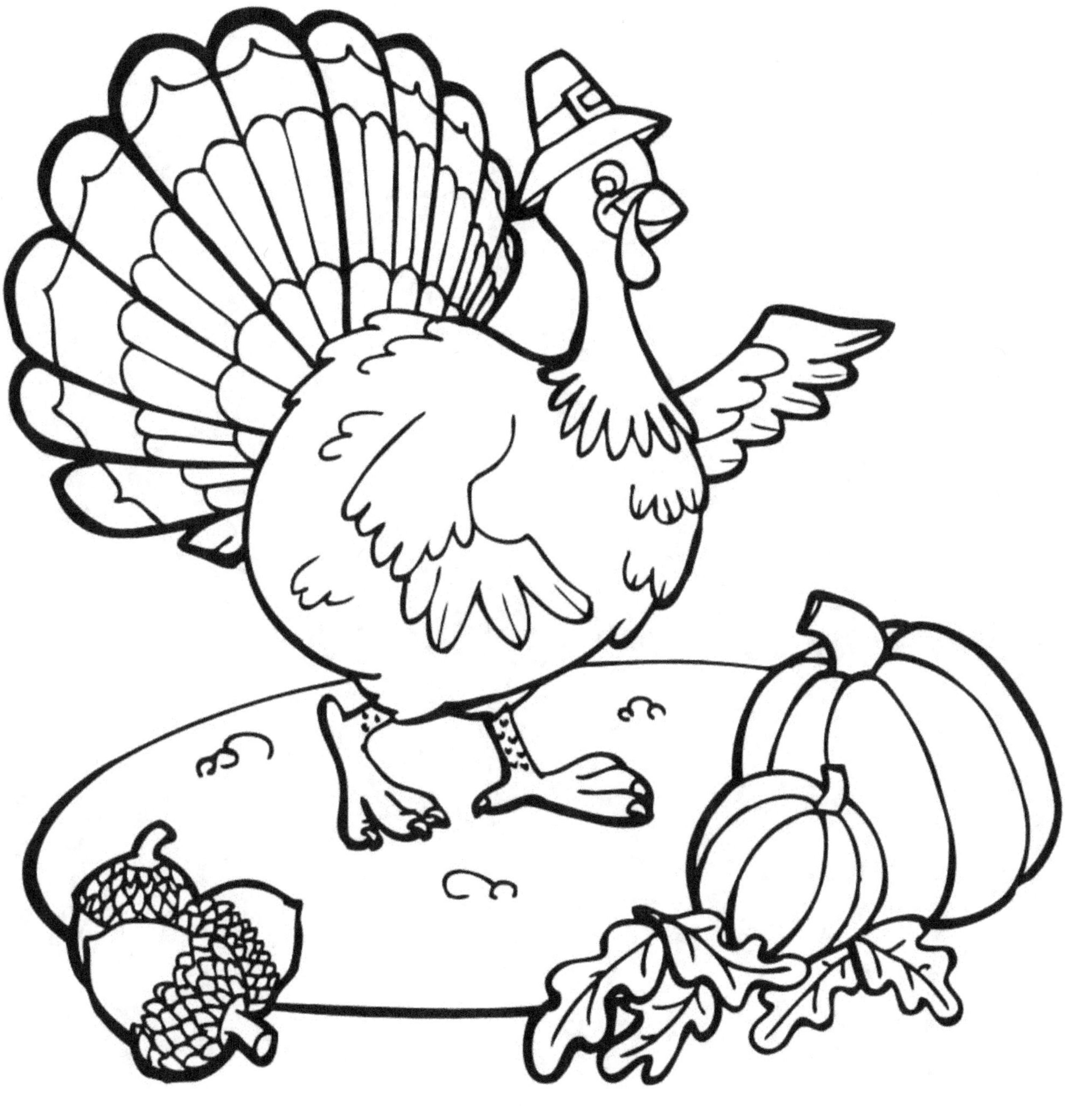

THANKSGIVING COLORING BOOK

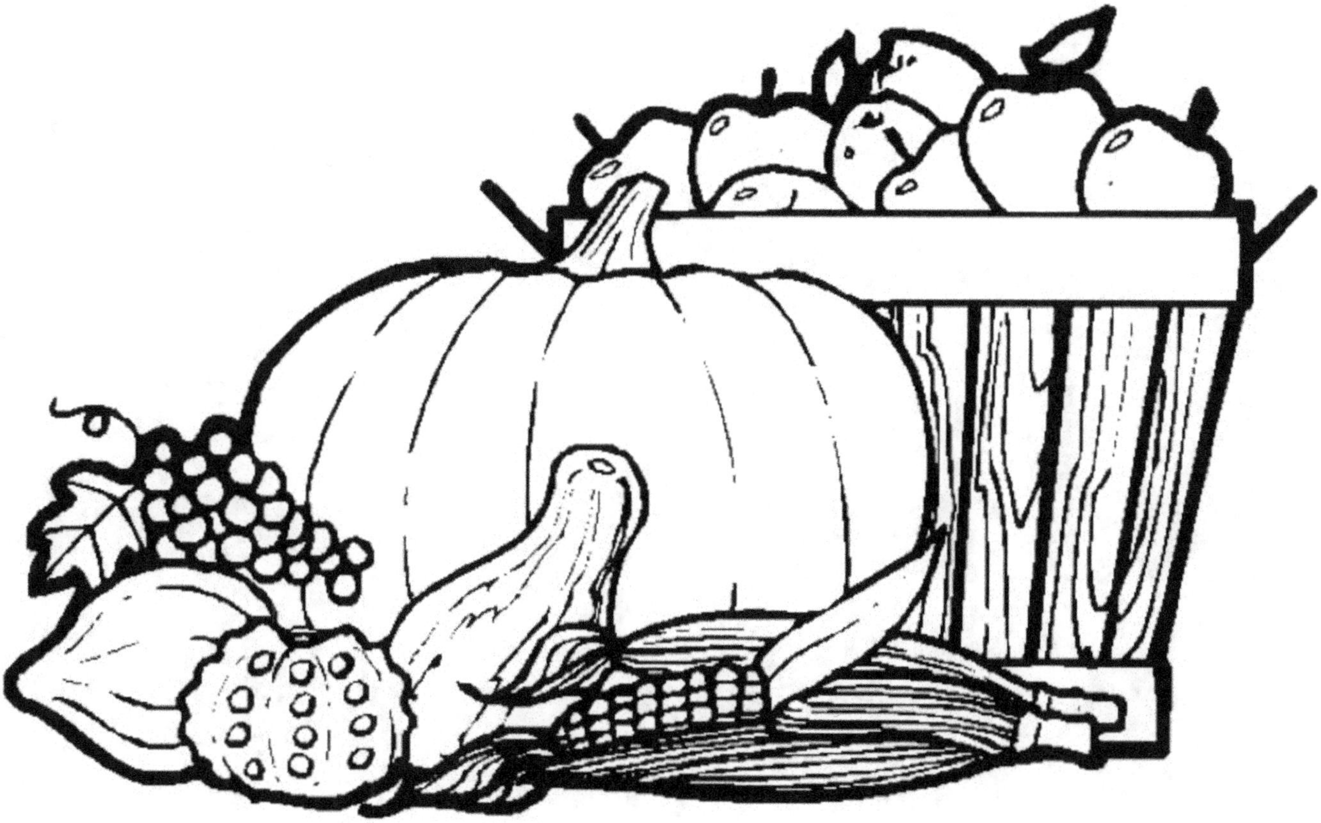

THANKSGIVING COLORING BOOK

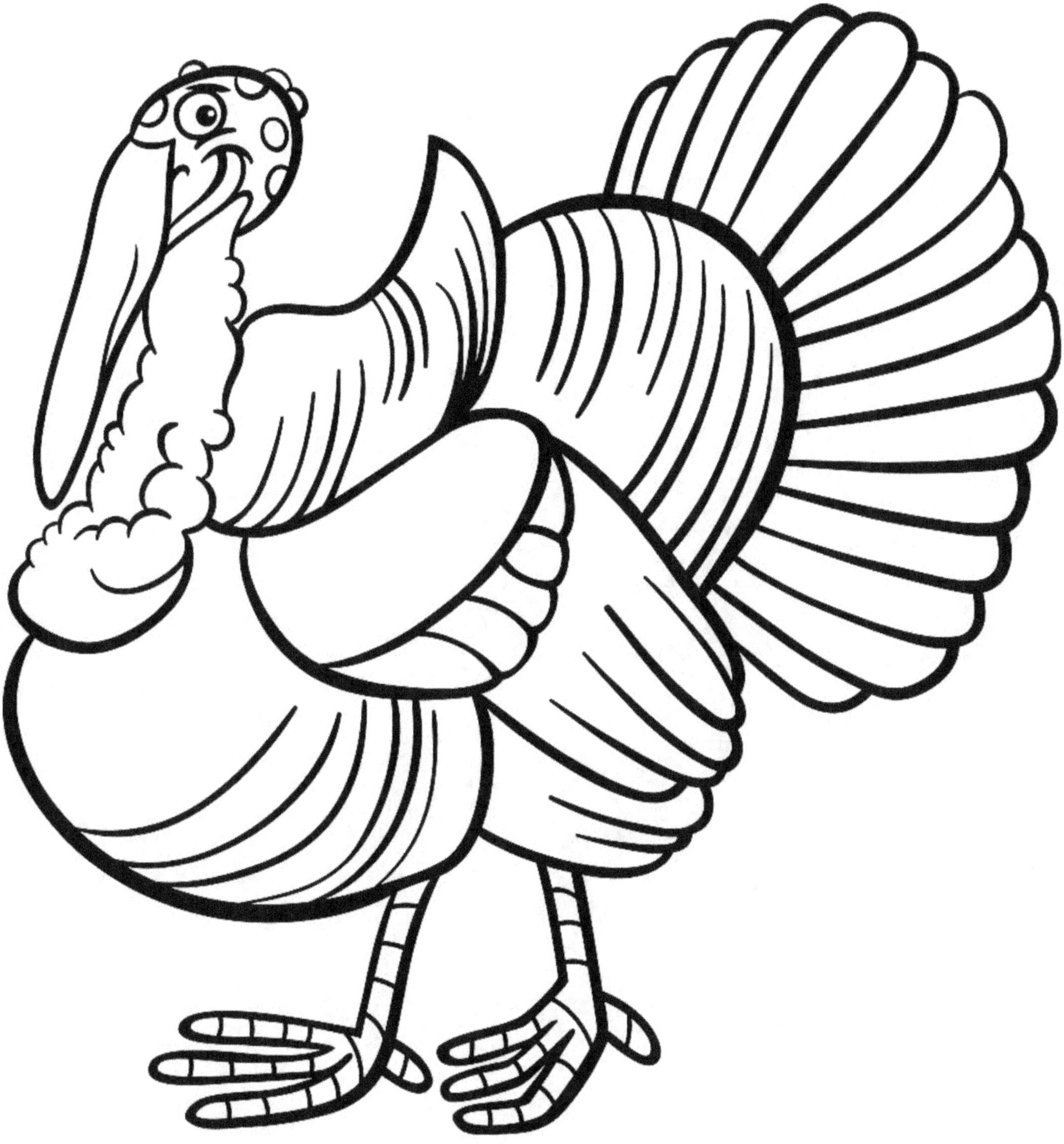

THANKSGIVING COLORING BOOK

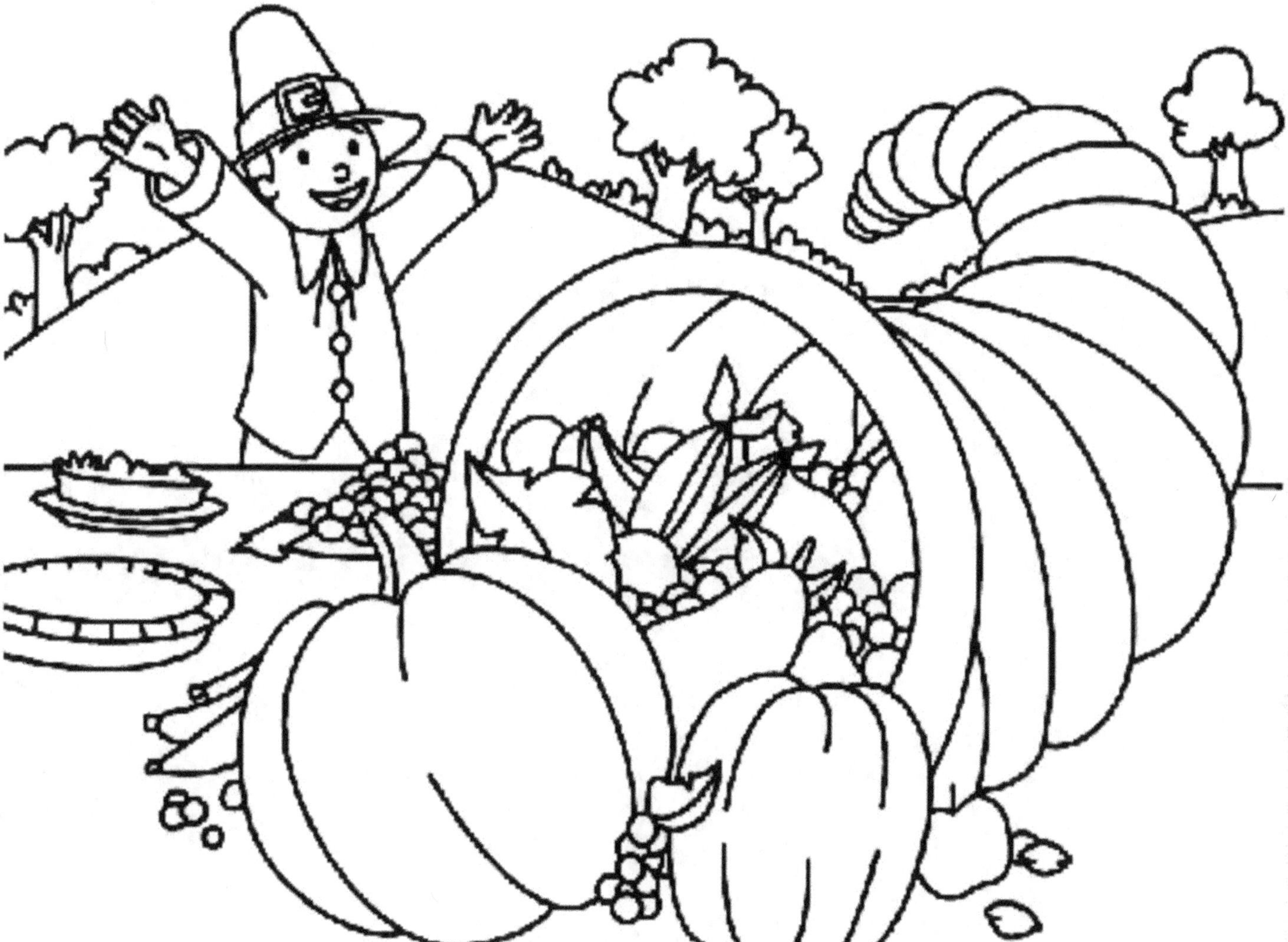

THANKSGIVING COLORING BOOK

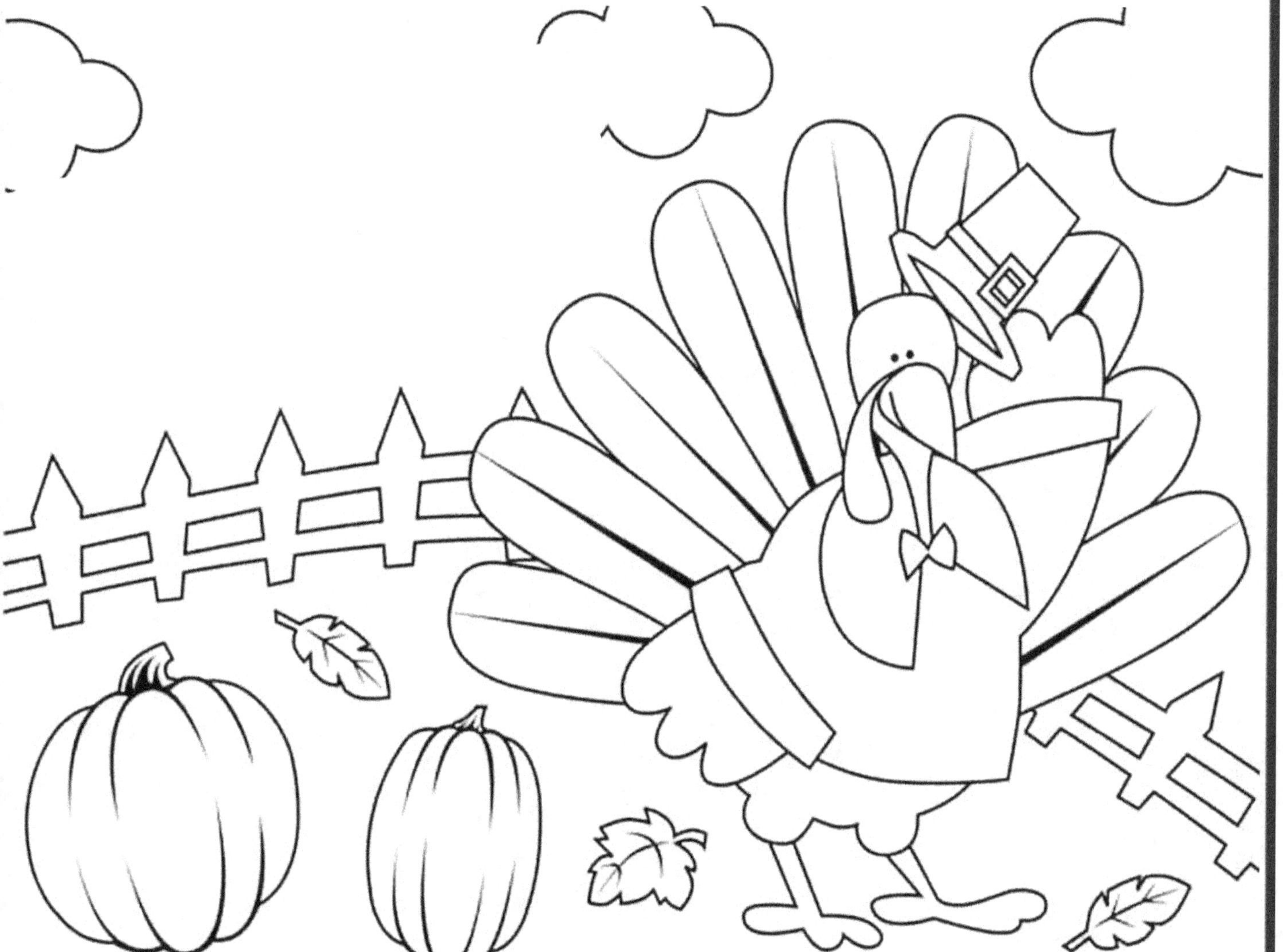

THANKSGIVING COLORING BOOK

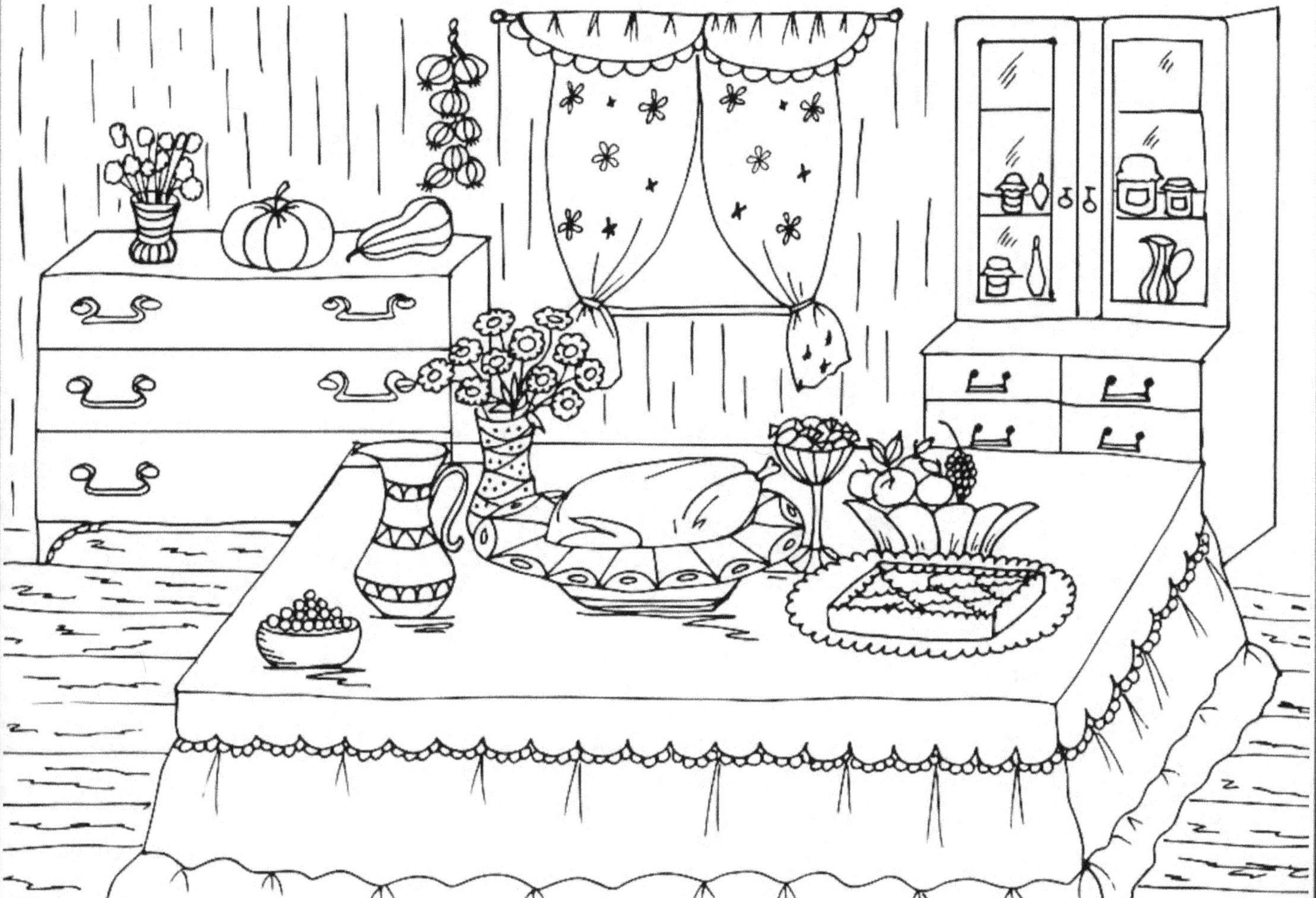

THANKSGIVING COLORING BOOK

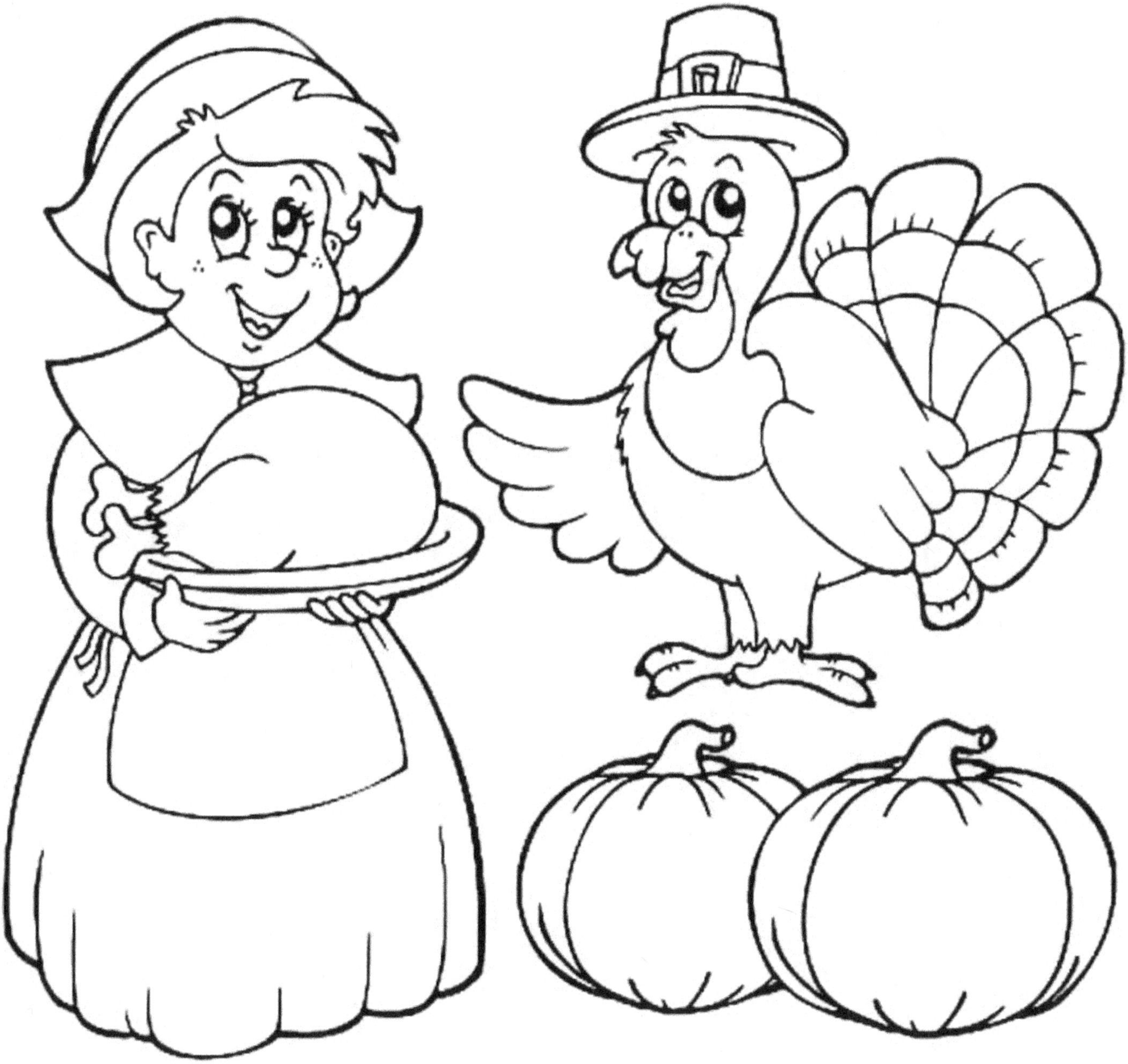

THANKSGIVING COLORING BOOK

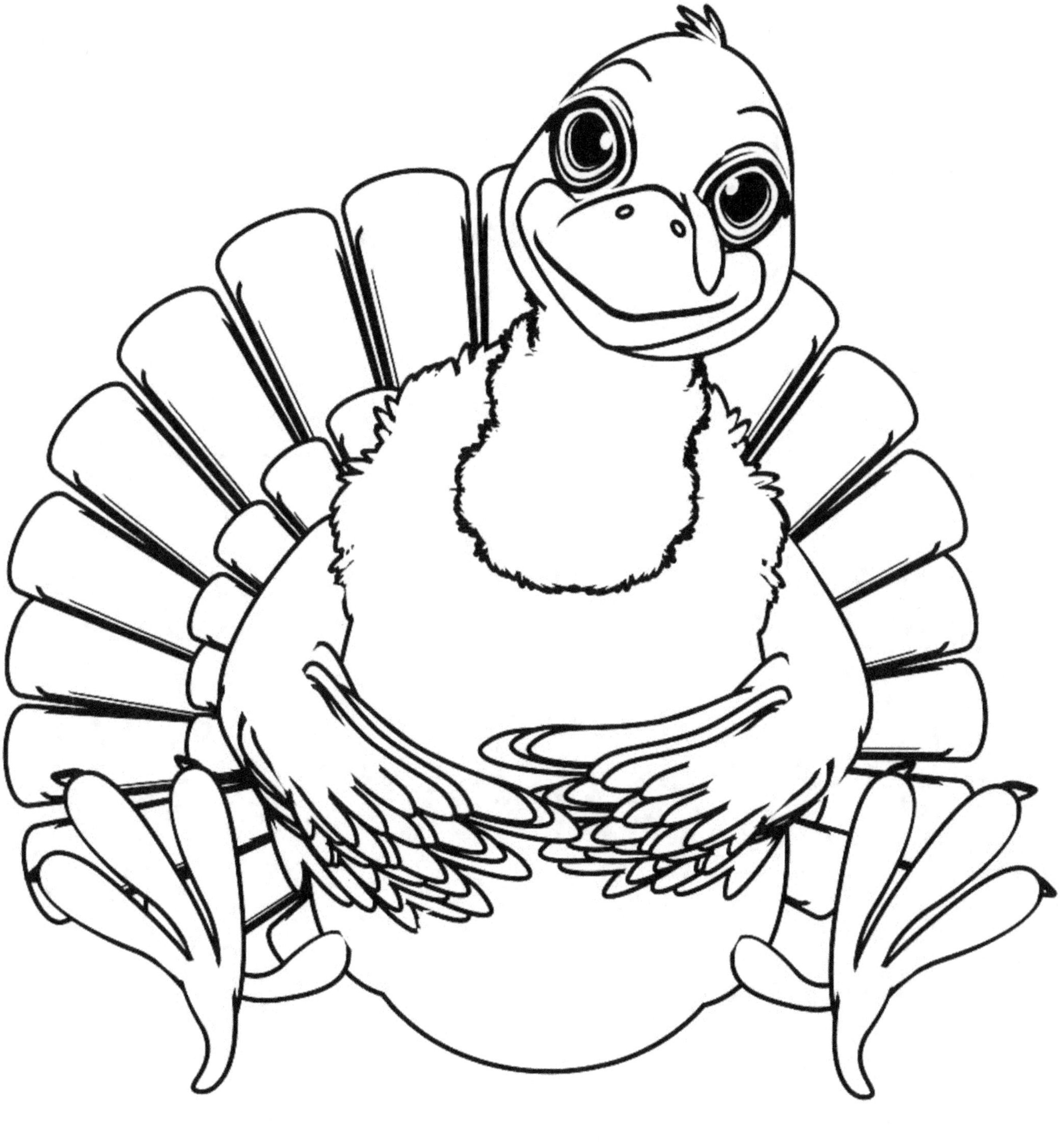

THANKSGIVING COLORING BOOK

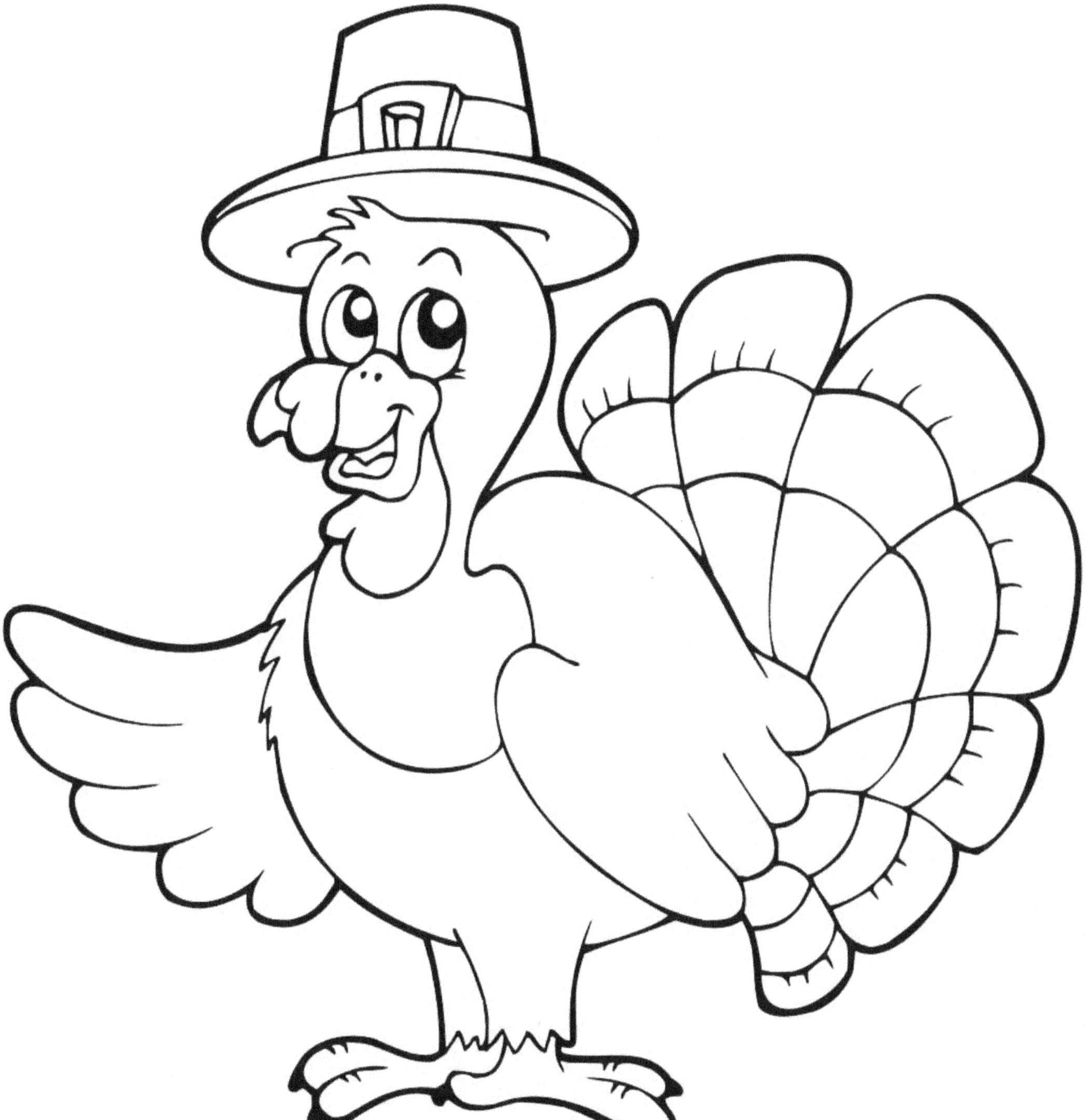

THANKSGIVING COLORING BOOK

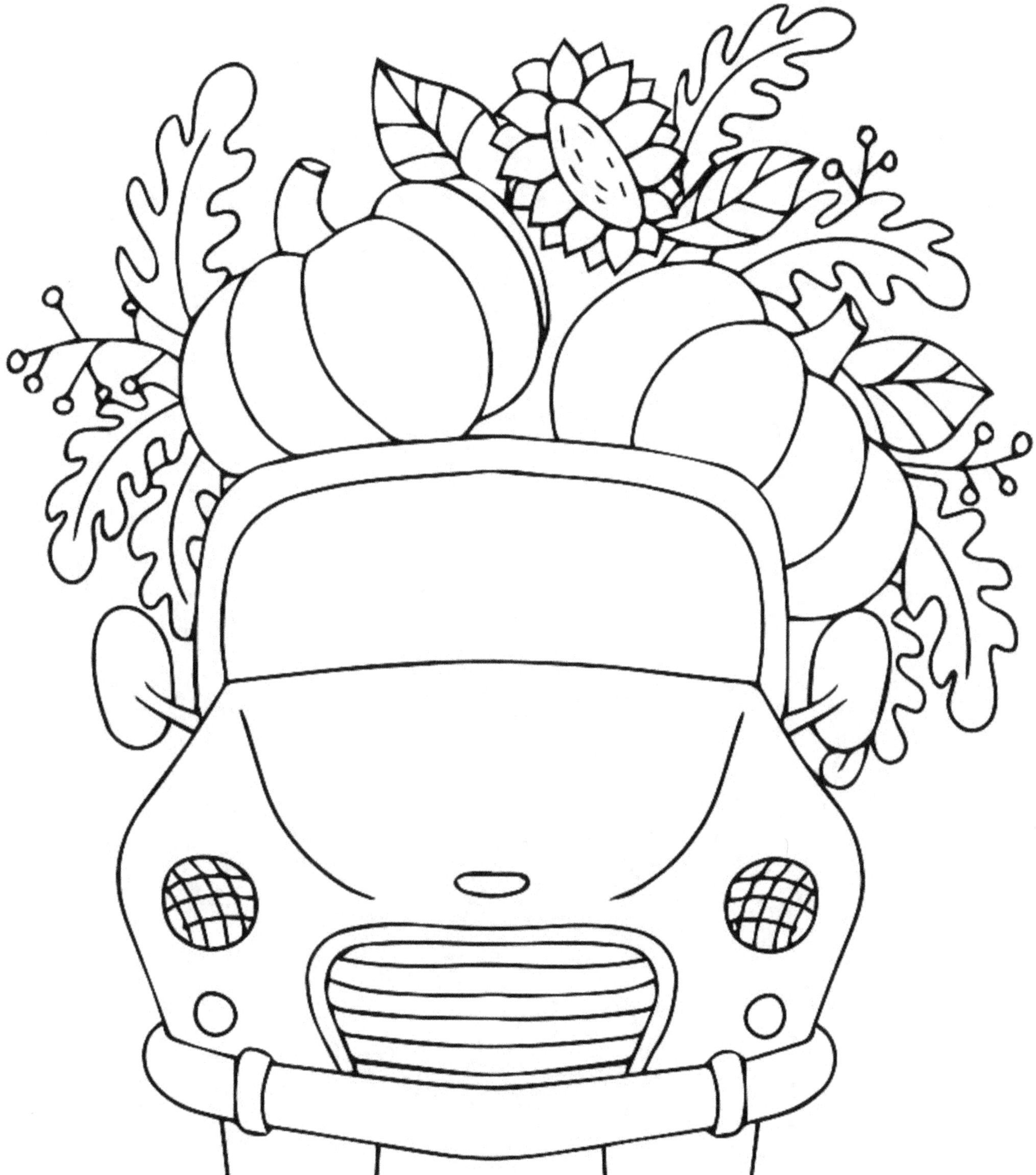

THANKSGIVING COLORING BOOK

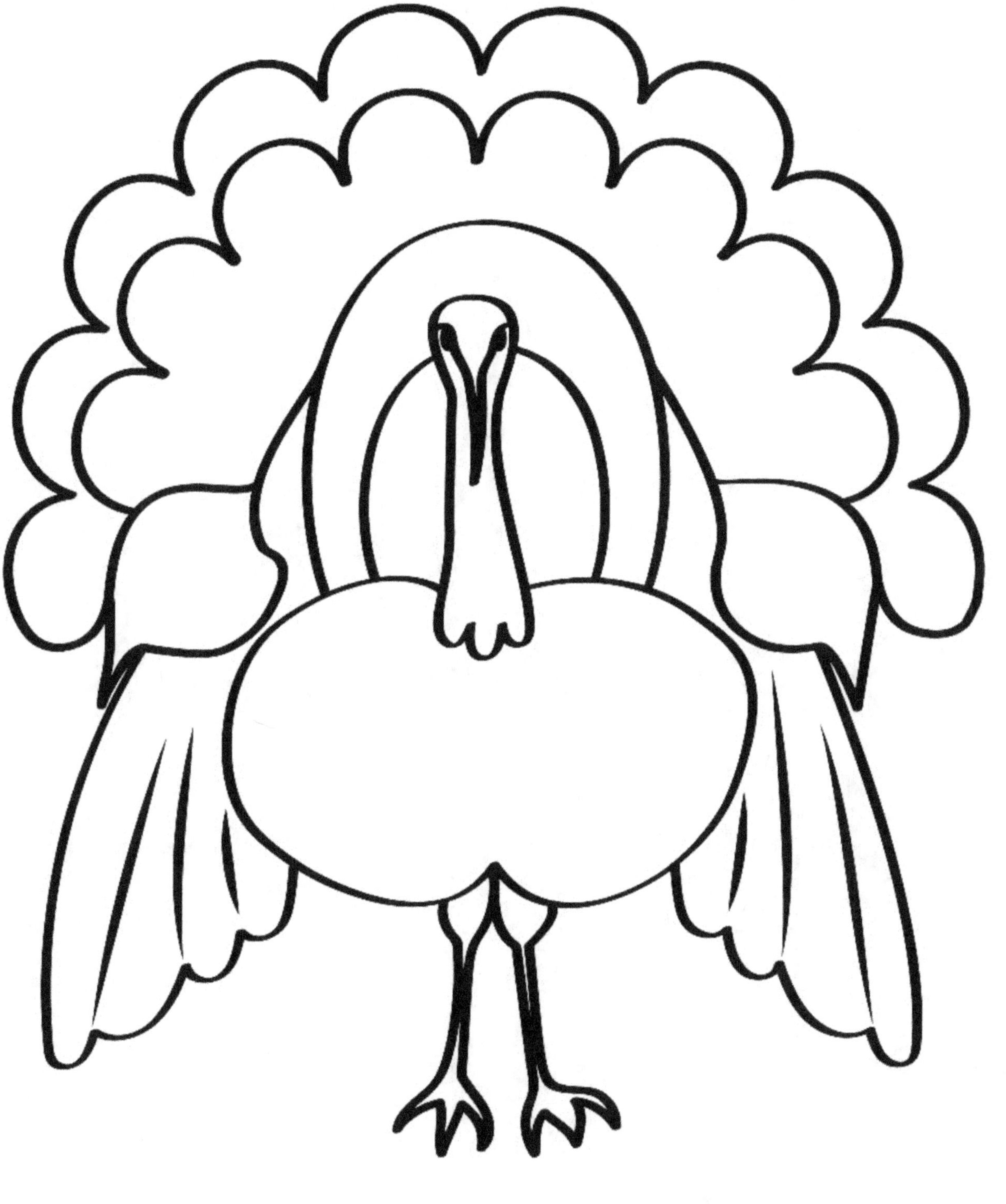

THANKSGIVING COLORING BOOK

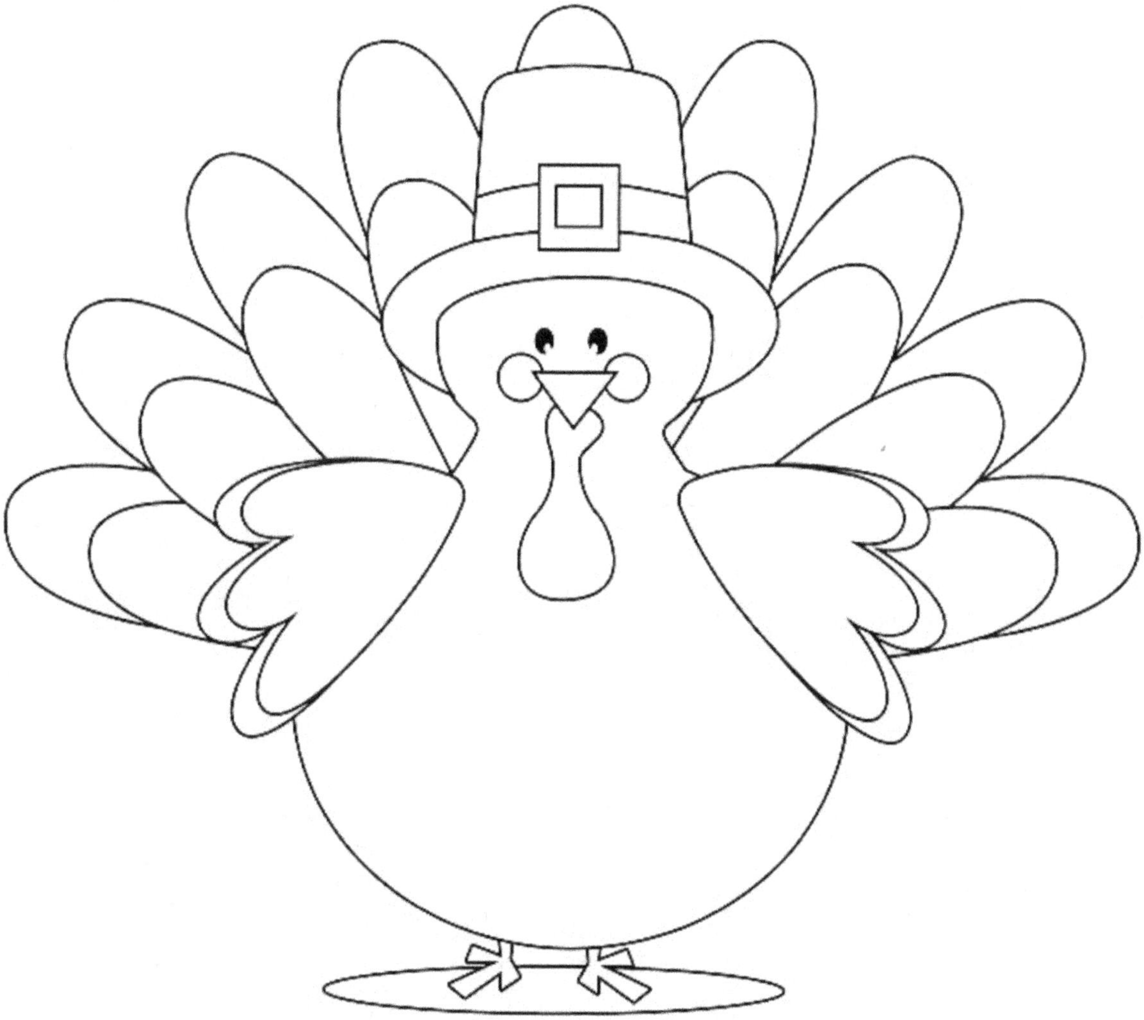

THANKSGIVING COLORING BOOK

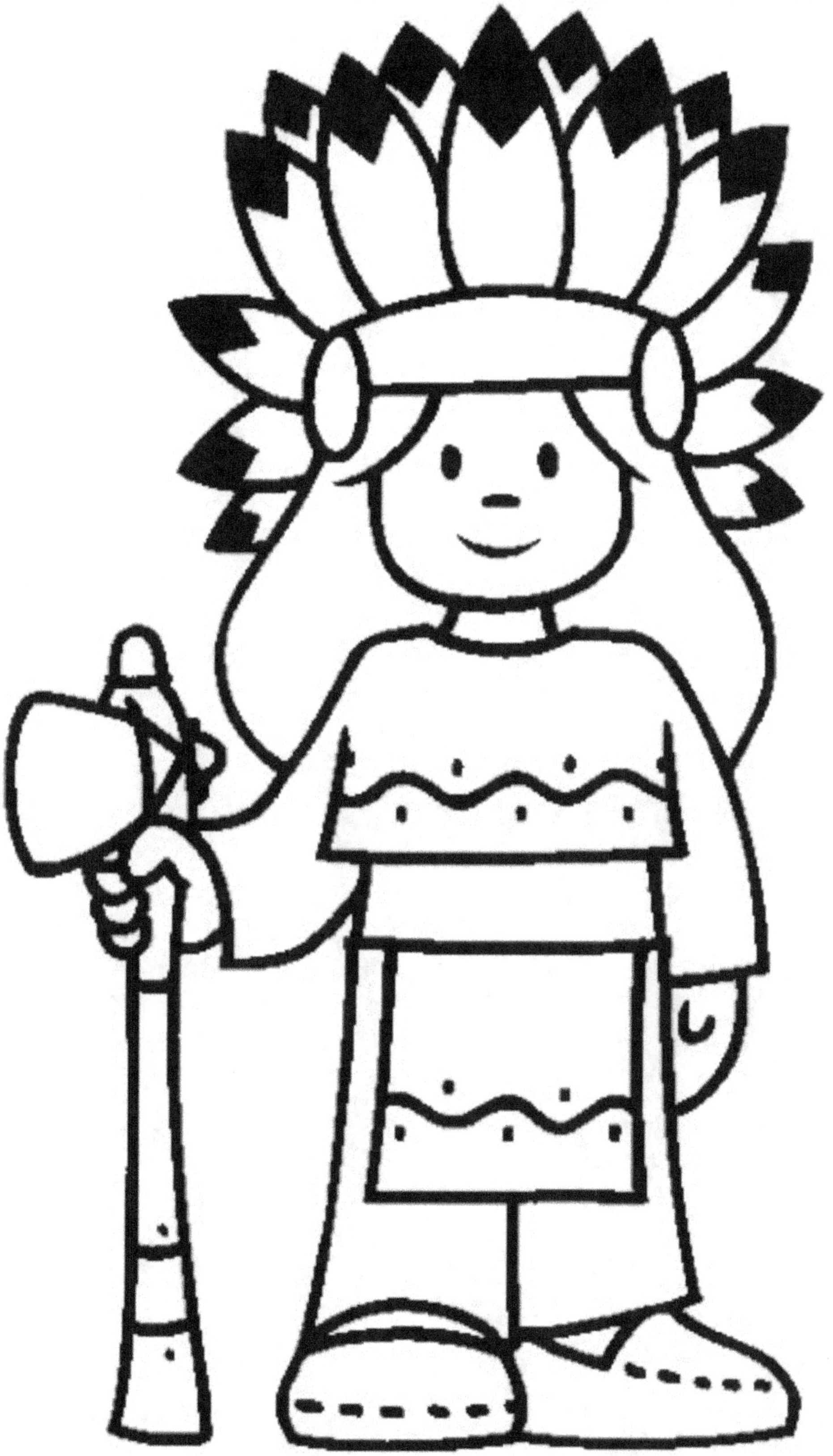

THANKSGIVING COLORING BOOK

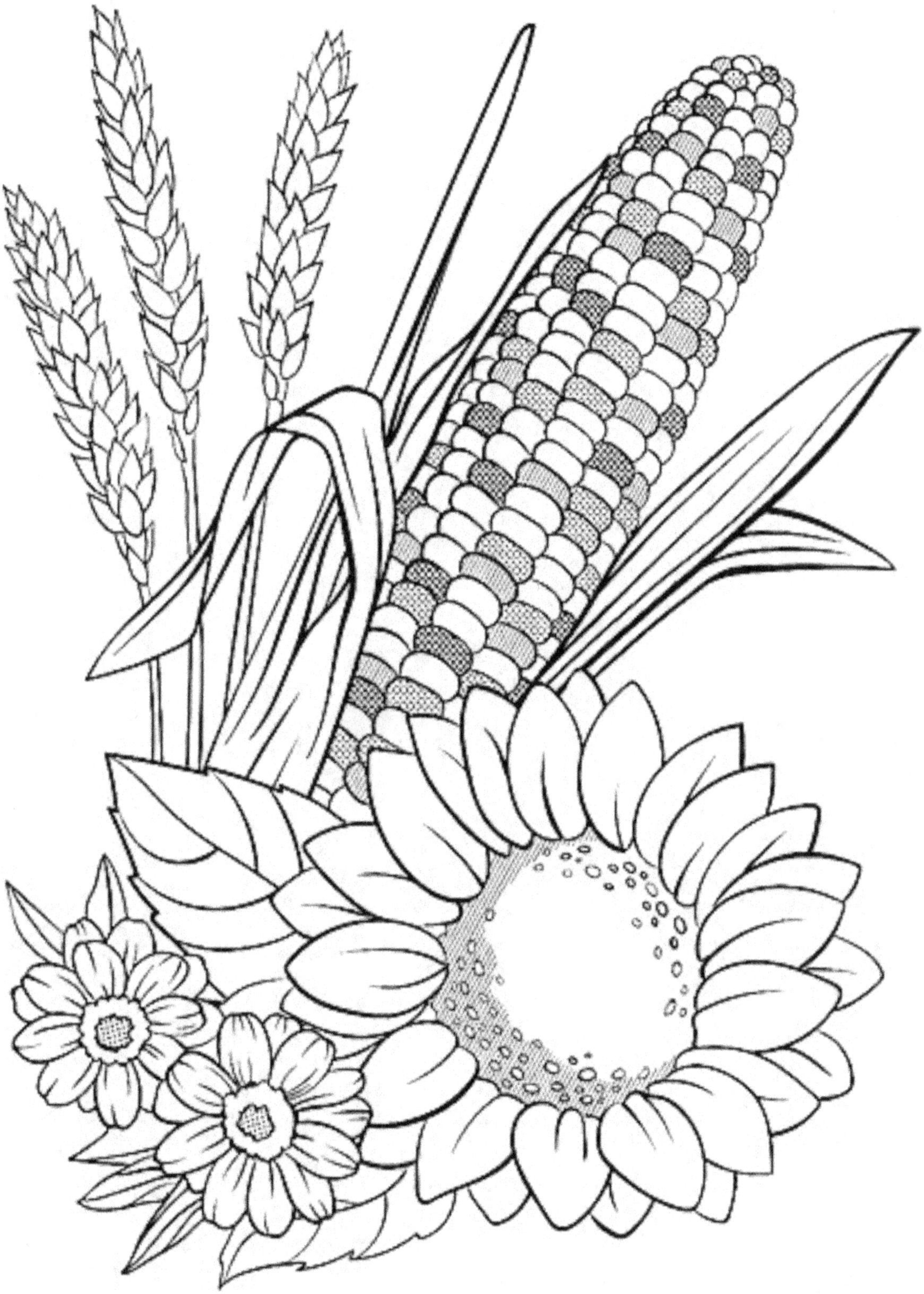

www.ingramcontent.com/pod-product-compliance
Lightning Source LLC
Chambersburg PA
CBHW081444220526
45466CB00008B/2504
9798555916211